Effective Preaching

About the author: Dan Hook is a priest of the Diocese of Toowoomba who lectures in pastoral theology and homiletics at St. Paul's National Seminary, Sydney, and is frequently invited by dioceses to speak to priests on effective preaching.

Effective Preaching

DAN HOOK

E. J. DWYER

First published 1991 by
E. J. Dwyer (Australia) Pty Ltd
3/32-72 Alice Street
Newtown NSW 2042
Australia

National Library of Australia
Cataloguing-in-Publication data

Hook, Dan, 1945–
    Effective preaching

    ISBN 0 85574 412 X

    1. Preaching. I. Title.

251

Cover designed by Trevor Hood
Typeset in 12/13pt Bembo by Post Typesetters, Brisbane, Australia
Printed in Singapore by Chong Moh Offset Printing, Private Limited.

Acknowledgments

The definition of ministry, in Ch. 1, taken from *Theology of Ministry*, by Thomas Franklin O'Meara, O.P., is used with the permission of Paulist Press, New York, U.S.A.

The story of the "Bag Lady" in Ch. 5, reprinted from "The Bag Lady" in *Angels to Wish By* by Joseph J. Jukinalis. Copyright © 1983 by Resource Publications Inc. 160 E. Virginia St., #290, San Jose, Ca. 95112.

The diagram of the Information Theory Triangle, in Ch. 7, taken from *Models of Theological Reflection* by Raymond Collins, is used with the permission of University Press of America, Lanham, Md. U.S.A.

Excerpts from the *Jerusalem Bible*, copyright © 1966 by Darton Longman & Todd Ltd. and Doubleday, a division of Bantam Doubleday Dell Publishing Group, Inc. Reprinted by Permission.

MY HOPE...

Good homilies happen when preachers
prepare well. My hope is that this book will
assist preachers to use their preparation
time effectively.

MY THANKS...

To my colleagues on the staff of St. Paul's
Seminary for their encouragement and
suggestions;

To Neville for his painstaking editing;

To Catherine Hammond and the staff at E.J. Dwyer's;

To my family and close friends, whose
support made completion of the book
possible.

FOR BILL,

A true preacher of the Word in
its fullness.

Contents

Contents

The Background to the Ministry

Preaching as Ministry

IN RECENT YEARS I have had the great pleasure of working with a group of men who were preparing for presbyteral ministry in the Catholic Church as a "second career". Many of these men had achieved significantly in their former work situations. They were accustomed to a busy schedule in their business and professional lives and were familiar with the demands of decision making and people management. After completing their formal studies, and before any final decisions about ordinations were made, they were required to undertake a pastoral placement designed to allow them to experience presbyteral ministry at first hand, or as close as possible, without actual ordination. While most found the time stimulating and enriching, all found that it was not without its difficulties.

One problem that many encountered is what I call the "tyranny of the immediate". So often they found it difficult to move quickly from one pastoral task to another. As well, they were at least surprised, and often amazed, at the range of human experience that is at the heart of day-to-day ministry in a parish. As one commented to me, "How do you ever get used to going from grieving with a family whose loved one died at 4 p.m., to sharing the joy and enthusiasm of a young couple about to be married at 6.30 p.m — and eat in between!"

Those of us who have ministered for any length of time in a local church know only too well what these men were encountering for the first time. But, given their previous experience in the business and professional world, the very fact that this aspect of the ministry proved difficult for most of them seems to warrant some further consideration.

To be effective in any job it is necessary to be able to focus our attention on the task at hand. In this, parish ministry is neither more nor less demanding than any other job. What does seem to set it apart from many other professions is the *context* and the *manner* in which the parish minister is called upon to focus upon the task at hand.

While no one would want to suggest that parish ministers dramatically move from one profound human experience to another, often enough they do find themselves involved with helping people to make meaning of the profound ordinariness of human living and dying. Being with people and sharing their experience at this level can not only be entirely consuming, but emotionally and physically draining.

Added to this, is the unpredictability of the daily workload. Someone once said, "Life is what happens when you have made other plans", and that is surely true of parish ministry. It is not unusual for the parish minister to have to deal with a wide range of human emotions in a matter of a few hours. Often, even usually, there is little or no warning as to what the person pressing the doorbell or on the other end of a ringing telephone wishes to speak about.

The demands of each immediate ministerial task require a good deal of psychic energy and as a result, at the end of the day, there may be little energy or inclination left for reflection. In such circumstances, it can happen that ministers begin to lose sight of the wider context in which they are exercising their ministry. They can become cynical about the value of wider considerations and dismiss them as theoretical or academic and of little or no value to them at the coalface. If this happens, then they have become *tyrannized by the immediate.* Their ministry can lack a depth and breadth of vision that can come only from appreciation and understanding of the history and development of Christian ministry throughout the ages.

I was reminded of this when I first visited the Melbourne Art Gallery. There I saw some of Frederick McCubbin's work for the first time. In one of his famous paintings I was struck by the two central figures who were sawing a log with a crosscut saw. The background was the Australian bush as only McCubbin was able to portray it. Then I noticed a third figure. Sitting a little away from the men was a woman nursing a baby. In noticing her, the whole painting changed for me and took on a new depth of meaning. Not only did I view the men differently, I also viewed the bush differently.

I believe much the same is true of ministry. Individual ministries are understood best when seen in their wider context. It is this context that helps to define and guide them. Reciprocally, individual ministries play a significant part in contributing to and shaping the broader context in which all ministries function. And so before we undertake a more detailed examination of the ministry of preaching, which will include a number of practical suggestions for the preparation of a homily, it is important that we first consider the wider context in which we practice the ministry of preaching.

Looking at the generic nature of ministry can shed light on the way the ministry of preaching is practiced today. In his excellent book, *A Theology of Ministry*, Thomas O'Meara, after a thorough study of the history and theology of ministry, offers the following definition of Christian ministry: "Christian ministry is the public activity of a baptized follower of Jesus Christ, flowing from the Spirit's charism and an individual personality, on behalf of a Christian community, to witness to, serve, and realize the Kingdom of God". From this definition, four interrelated observations seem relevant in helping to focus our understanding of the ministry of preaching.

a)   The definition makes the point that every ministry flows from baptism. Consequently, they all bear the mark of this most fundamental Christian sacrament.

Essentially, baptism is the ritual that celebrates a person becoming part of a Christian community. In asking for baptism, individuals commit themselves to the Christian way of life espoused by the community. In accepting the new member, the Christian community commits itself to nurture and support the member in living a life faithful to the attitudes and values which guided and directed the life of Jesus himself. It is from the community that an individual learns what is at the heart of Christian living, and it is from within the Christian community that a person is inspired and empowered to live the Christian values. The Christian endeavor, from both an individual and a community point of view, is then very much about a way of living, about a way of making meaning of the ordinary human experience that is the stuff of life.

This is the context for the ministry of preaching, as indeed it is

5

for all ministry. Preaching is essentially about a *way of living*. It is about making meaning of our ordinary human experience in the light of the attitudes and values contained in the gospel. As such it needs to be eminently *practical*. It seeks to articulate a way of life which is *lived*, not simply hypothesized about. If the ministry is to be effective, then ministers will need to be thoroughly conversant with the actual lives being lived by those with whom they minister. What is more, ministers need a thorough understanding of the processes of nurture, guidance and support that the community offers to its members. As well, of course, they need to be aware of and capable of interpreting human experience in terms of the gospel. Each of these skills will be addressed in subsequent chapters.

b) By seeing ministry as "flowing from the Spirit's charism and an individual personality", O'Meara revives memories of the old theological principle that "grace builds on nature". Every individual brings a unique personality and giftedness to the community. St Paul maintains that it is through these individual gifts and abilities that the Spirit incarnates itself in the lives of individual people. These "Spirit infused" abilities he terms "charisms", and it is these gifts that are the basis of the various ministries needed within the community so that it might achieve its basic aims and goals. Naturally, different people have different gifts and a person is never called to a ministry that is not consistent with his or her personal gifts.

These gifts are always exercised within a community. It is important, then, that not only should individuals own and acknowledge their personal giftedness, but that this same giftedness be recognized and acknowledged by the community. This interaction is crucial. It can sometimes happen that an individual may genuinely believe they are gifted for a particular ministry when it is obvious to the community that this is not the case. On the other hand, sometimes the community can recognize a person's gifts while he or she is blind to them. The proper discernment of these gifts is integral to the fulfillment of both the individual and the community. If the individual fails to use his or her gifts, the active presence of the Spirit in their lives is restricted. If the community fails to use the gifts of its members, to some extent it will fail in incarnating the Kingdom, for it truly lives only in its members.

Once people have offered their gifts to the community, and the community has affirmed these gifts, it then becomes the responsibility of the community to encourage and nurture them. At the appropriate time, the community authorizes the individual to exercise these gifts in the fulfillment of the community's mission, and provides that person with all the training and support needed for their effective use.

The ordination and designation rituals of the various Christian traditions are the traditional ways in which local churches affirm the presence in individuals of the gift of preaching. Unfortunately, we all know that it sometimes happens that people are confirmed in this ministry who lack the personal giftedness to effectively exercise it. While ordination or designation rituals may legislate a person to preach, they can never empower someone who does not have the natural Spirit-infused charism. Obviously, if preaching is to be an integral part of the leadership ministry within the local church, then those who are entrusted with this ministry must clearly manifest their giftedness before they are authorized to exercise the ministry. Not to seriously discern this gift, either on the part of the individual or the community, will be to the detriment of both.

Since charisms are uniquely personal, it stands to reason that each community-designated preacher will bring to the ministry a unique personal slant. Put succinctly, while there is *no one way* to preach, for each individual there is *only one way*! To surrender this uniqueness by using homilies essentially prepared by others, however insightful, is to surrender responsibility for the ministry with which the person has been entrusted. As well, a minimal use of charismatic gifts frustrates the creative presence of the Spirit in the lives of both the individual and the community.

This charismatic characteristic of ministry also raises the topical question of who can be gifted. In the Catholic tradition, at present the exercise of the ministry of preaching is restricted to ordained presbyters and deacons. The question of the justice of this position has been argued extensively. In terms of the Spirit-infused gifts necessary for preaching, it would seem clear that these exist in people and are not restricted to gender or lifestyle. If the Spirit incarnates itself in our world through the exercise of people's charisms, any legislative position that restricts their authentic use would again seem to restrict the creative presence of the Spirit in our world.

c) O'Meara points out that Christian ministry is the "public activity... on behalf of the community". Contained within this characteristic of ministry lie responsibilities for both minister and community. All ministry belongs not to the minister, but to the community. Consequently, it is the responsibility of the community to ensure the effectiveness of the ministry.

From the ministers' point of view, this requires them to be aware that they do not exercise this ministry for their own personal satisfaction or sanctification. While the effective exercise of the ministry will contribute greatly to their own personal fulfillment as Christians, they must be aware that their ministry is always at the service of the community and accountable to the community.

This consideration becomes relevant in the choice of content for homilies. Preachers need to ensure that they are addressing issues relevant to the community with whom they are ministering, and not simply to their own personal agendas. As well, it seems reasonable for the community to have some means whereby it is able to express its opinion as to the effectiveness of the ministry. It behooves the minister to listen carefully to what the community says about the effectiveness of the ministry.

From the community's point of view, taking responsibility for the effectiveness of the ministry involves nurturing, supporting and affirming their ministers. As well, it involves providing them with opportunities to sharpen their skills through ongoing education and training, along with provision of the "tools of trade" necessary for effective exercise of the ministry within the local church. My experiences with local churches throughout Australia would indicate that most communities (and most clergy) still see the ministry of preaching as belonging personally to the presbyter and hence would be unaware of any responsibilities they have as a community with respect to this.

The best way in which a community can ensure the effectiveness of the ministry of preaching is to have it exercised by a competent minister. Present practices and attitudes within local churches often undermine the competence of the preaching minister. Preaching is a reflective ministry. The minister is called to dialogue between the lived experience of the community and the gospel. *This takes time!* In many communities such time is not available because of the other demands placed on the preaching minister, either through his or her own expectations or the expectations of the community.

People often complain about the quality of homilies in their parish, but are reluctant to offer their own giftedness in order to fulfill some of the ministries presently being fulfilled by their preacher. It would seem that it is a responsibility of the community to ensure that the minister has time to exercise the ministry effectively.

Preaching is a skill which can always be improved. To this end, ongoing education is essential if a minister is to maintain effectiveness over a long period. From time to time conferences and seminars will be offered and for some this will provide much needed nourishment. It would seem appropriate for the community to provide the wherewithal for their minister to attend these. However, most will nourish themselves for the ministry through reading. I believe that in practical terms, the community has a significant role to play in the provision of this nourishment. On present salaries many ministers are unable to buy the books and magazines that they need. If addressing the salary situation is beyond the competence of the local church, it would seem essential for the preacher to be provided with a book allowance.

In preaching, it is not so much what is said that is important as what is heard; and in many churches very little can be heard because of poor sound equipment. Something as simple as this can undermine an otherwise effective preaching ministry. A preacher does have the right to efficient tools of trade!

d)   O'Meara sees the goal of all ministry as "to witness to, serve, and realize the Kingdom of God". Immediately we are confronted with the question as to what is the Kingdom of God and how is it made present.

As with Jesus in the gospel, the only way we are able to gain some understanding of the Kingdom is through analogy. Sometimes we hear the phrase "that is his or her kingdom". What this tries to express is that in that particular area, be it within a home or an office, everything that happens somehow or other bears the "mark" of that person. Similarly, the Kingdom of God exists in our world where human experience somehow bears the "mark of God". It is through the revelation made known in Jesus and handed down through generations of faithful Christian believers that we are able to gain insight into how the human person acts when under the influence of this Reign of God. Where this Reign exists, people are able to fulfill their full potential as humans. Obviously, this

9

Reign of God involves a political and social dimension as well as a comprehensive understanding of how to make meaning of, and effectively respond to, human experience.

The local church is called to serve, witness to and realize this Kingdom. It does this firstly through living its own community life in such a way that the Reign of God and its freedom is experienced by its members. In so doing, it begins to realize the Kingdom and become its sacrament. Out of this experience, and as a part of it, the church is then called to affirm where the Kingdom is present in our world and point to where it is absent.

As an integral part of the whole ministry of the local church, the ministry of preaching shares these same aims and goals. In many ways, the preacher is called to be the voice of the community in announcing the presence or absence of the Kingdom. As such it is a political ministry, as much aware of the world environment as it is of the state of the local community life.

This requires of the minister the skills to be able to critically reflect upon the state of our world, and bring the forces dominating that world under the gaze of the values and attitudes of the gospel. To speak this truth requires courage and fortitude, especially when the preacher is called to point to the absence of the Kingdom, whether at a personal, community or societal level. Such courage is probably only available to the preacher who is absolutely convinced that in Jesus and his Kingdom lie the means of human fulfillment.

Preaching as Revelation

WHAT IS ACTUALLY happening in the preaching event? Essentially, preachers are trying to facilitate some sort of liberating encounter between the believer and God. They are aiming to bring the lives of individuals and communities into dialogue with the Word of God. Their task is about uncovering the already present Spirit in the life experience of the individuals and the community to whom they minister. In essence, then, they are really ministering the process of revelation. An examination of this can help us to sharpen our understanding of the ministry of preaching.

The actual theology of revelation out of which we live will substantially affect our style of preaching. Broadly, it could be said that we adopt either a deductive or an inductive model of revelation. Each of these approaches has a different "feel" and it has been my experience that people become aware of their *actual* preferred model of revelation more by feel than from a conceptual discussion. While most will probably find their lived theology of revelation contains characteristics of both models, usually there is a disposition towards one model rather than the other. A broad pen picture of each model is enough to give us a clue as to which is our preference.

A *deductive* approach to revelation tends to see God as revealing a set of truths that become the infallible and unchangeable guidelines according to which the Christian is expected to live. The means of this revelation can vary. Some would propose that God infuses the revelation in the mind of the writer. Others would see that the insights disclosed by the writer are guaranteed by the authority of the Church through its teaching office. As well, there can be a variety of emphases upon the content. Protestant traditions will tend to emphasize the Scriptures as the primary content of revelation while, until recent times, the Catholic tradition has stressed the authenticating role of the teaching office of the Church and its tradition.

On one hand, the strength of this model is its respect for the collective wisdom accrued by faithful Christian communities over the centuries. No one generation has the capacity to appreciate the fullness of the liberating message revealed in Jesus of Nazareth. A deductive approach to revelation tends to encourage the present faith community to look at how Christian communities have lived the Christian life in various circumstances in history. This approach usually does this by focusing on the actual expressions of the Christian truths that these various Christian communities have made. In this way it protects the present Christian community from becoming obsessed with its own generation or local circumstances.

On the other hand, the model can fall prey to a number of difficulties. Because of its stress on the distilled wisdom of the past, often expressed in "credal" or "doctrinal" form, it can tend to emphasize a belief system heavily based upon reason. While reason will always play an integral role in the life of the Christian, there is a significant area of the Christian life that goes beyond reasonable explanation. As Pascal said, "The heart has its reasons of which the reason knows nothing", and in many ways the truth of the Christian message is a truth known by the heart.

This approach runs the risk of becoming arrogant in its presentation of the Christian truth by presuming to be able to speak with absolute authority in all things human and expect an obedient response. Because of its bias towards the conceptual presentation of the Christian message, the approach can also fall prey to a debilitating idealism. The Christian life can be seen in terms of how it ought to be. This ideal is projected from the inherited revealed truths and will usually be seen to be impossible to achieve.

Preachers living out of this model of revelation will be influenced, often unconsciously, by the model. Many will tend to see the ministry in terms of communicating a revealed truth. They will have a more didactic approach to preaching and consequently will be more conceptual in their content. Their better homilies will be marked by a clarity of thinking and a logical development that their listeners will appreciate. They will probably understand their authority to preach in terms of their office rather than personal charism, and this may inhibit their effort to develop their own giftedness. While every effort will be made to nuance their message for their hearers, because of a perceived need to conserve and be faithful to past revelation, it can happen that many homilies spend a good deal of time answering questions people never ask.

Because of the idealism inherent in this model, often preachers will use these ideals to elicit a guilt-filled response from their hearers. While such a response may be "effective" in the short term, it is difficult to see how guilt can be an authentic path to a Kingdom that is about liberation and freedom.

An *inductive* model of revelation has its own strengths and weaknesses. The fundamental assumption of this model is that God in his Spirit is constantly breaking in on our world. The spirit that enthused the historical Jesus is now at work in the lives of people, inviting them to live, in the present, the values and attitudes that shaped the way he lived in his day. By listening to this Spirit presence, which is at once totally within and yet beyond our human experience, we are invited and empowered to fulfill our human potential to love. The historical Jesus is the ultimate paradigm of fulfilled human potential. What connects us to Jesus is sharing the same Spirit.

The great strength of this model is its relevance for the world in which we live. It values human experience as the primary means of revelation, and encourages people to listen carefully to their own experience and trust the revealing presence of God which is at the heart of that experience. Authority within the model lies in the accuracy with which it is able to describe and make sense of ordinary human experience. It is more concerned with a certainty "of the heart" than "of the head", although this does not infer it is in any way unreasonable.

While the stress the model lays upon human experience is its great strength, it can also be its Achilles heel. It can easily fall prey to subjectivism and individualism. While people living out of this model usually value the Scripture, it sometimes happens that they undervalue the historical tradition of the Church, usually because of a reluctance to study the tradition in its proper historical context. Indeed, this attitude can also contribute to a subjective interpretation of the scriptural text which manifests a lack of understanding of its cultural and textual setting.

Preachers living out of this model will be influenced by it in significant ways. Obviously, in their homilies, they will concern themselves with human experience. Not only will this influence the content of their homilies, but it will also influence the way they see the preaching act itself. In the main they will be trying to facilitate an actual experience of the Spirit during the homily, rather than trying to communicate particular ideas. Usually their listeners will appreciate what they have to say as it will be addressing many of the issues of their day-to-day life. Good preachers will tend to be people who are able to listen critically to their own experience, and the experience of their communities, within the atmosphere of the Spirit of the Scriptures and the tradition of the Church.

Without such reflection the preaching ministry can become fairly superficial. This has happened in the recent past. In seeking relevance, some preachers have become slaves of popular psychologies and their homilies have tended to depend more upon the power of psychology than the power of the Spirit and the Word.

Regardless of which model people live out of, all would agree that the revelatory process requires an individual to be disposed to hear and respond to the presence of the Spirit in his or her life. The Spirit does not force itself upon people. More often than not, it gently invites them to wholeness. As a midwife of this process, the preacher needs to be careful not to be more forceful than God. It is his or her responsibility to simply invite people to adult faith.

Revelation involves what may be termed an "event–word" process. It entails a human experience being interpreted by the Word of God. Scripture, which is seen as the normative expression of revelation in Jesus, happened as the result of this process.

The pattern of development that issued in our present scriptural texts could be outlined as follows: it began with Jesus' personal human experience. He brought to this his own unique insight that sprang from his being God become human. As a person experiencing the human condition he interpreted in an entirely new way what it meant to be human. In what he said and the way he acted, Jesus lived out this new interpretation of how to be human.

It was this insight that he shared with his disciples, and as a result of their association with him, the disciples too began to live differently. Through him they found a new Spirit within themselves.

The truth of this new interpretation was ultimately tested in Jesus' death. Incredibly, the disciples found that after his death, the

Spirit of Jesus lived on, and that it offered to those who responded to it the same liberation and freedom that they had experienced by being in the presence of Jesus himself. The ever-present Spirit now triggered the memory of the historical Jesus who had revealed to them an all loving, all forgiving God. In this knowledge, people were able to live life freely.

As their various experiences within their communities triggered different memories of the historical Jesus, the oral tradition, that is at the heart of the written gospels, gradually took shape. Several generations later, the evangelists themselves interpreted the experiences of their own communities in the light of this oral tradition and wrote it down in a form close to that which we today know as the gospels.

In the development of the gospel text, there are three distinct contributing sources: the oral tradition, the community of the evangelist, and the evangelists themselves. The text was born out of the dynamic interaction of these sources. This process could be visualized as follows:

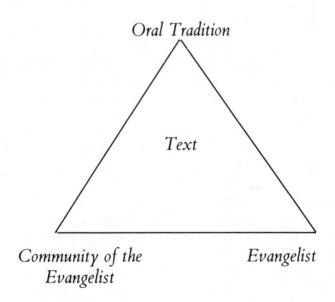

Oral Tradition

Text

Community of the
Evangelist

Evangelist

This process gives a clue to the sources of the content of homilies. Since the homily ministers the process of revelation, it becomes the interpreting word for the human experiences of individuals and communities.

The triangle that describes the development of our gospel texts is just as applicable to the development of the Sunday homily:

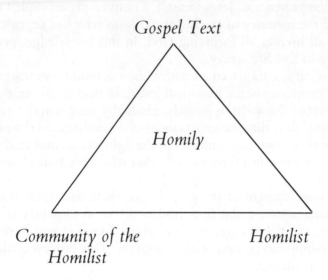

Gospel Text

Homily

*Community of the
Homilist*   *Homilist*

It is within the interaction of these three poles that a good homily is born. Each of the poles is essential. Without considering the experience of the community, we risk becoming irrelevant; without considering our own faith experience, we risk becoming insincere; without considering the text, we risk preaching a gospel other than that of Christ.

The revelation process primarily discloses not so much the nature of the Revealer/God, but the *relationship* between God and humans. From within the revelatory experience, we gain a heightened awareness of how we are in relationship with God, and it is out of this that we are empowered to live differently. It is from this experience of relationship that we can begin to understand the nature of the Revealer/God. Ultimately, changing human behavior is the goal of all revelation.

Again, this aspect of the revelation process gives us some important clues for preaching. Like every other form of revelation, the focus of the ministry needs to be on the facilitation of an experience of the relationship between God and his people. It is only when people have experienced this relationship that they will feel empowered to live out its implications in their everyday life. While knowledge about God can help people understand their relationship with God better, it will rarely provide the motivation and enthusiasm needed for effective conversion. Preachers need to be on their guard against using the homily as a means for adult education. The primary objective of the ministry is to help people experience their relationship with God, *as the homily is actually being delivered.*

Finally, revelation is a social process. It involves individuals bringing their personal experience to be tested and authenticated by a community of believers who share with them a common interest in living a life in the Spirit. There is an ongoing interaction between the experience of the individual and the experience of the community. The community nurtures and guides the individual to live in such a way that they are disposed to respond to the inbreaking of God in their lives. At the same time, the life of the community itself is enriched and substantially shaped by the experiences of its individual members.

This social dimension of the process of revelation points to the need for the ministry of preaching to be integrated with a number of other ministries and activities in the community. While preaching may provide the "trigger" for people to reflect upon their own experience and that of their community, this "triggering" needs to be complemented with opportunities within the community for more extended reflection. Prayer groups and Scripture discussion groups are the most common ways in which people are encouraged. Unfortunately, many communities lack structures which allow them to reflect upon their communal life. Where community reflection is not a part of a community's life, it often happens that the preaching ministry fails to address communal needs and challenge communal attitudes and values. Without this dimension, the ministry of preaching runs the risk of becoming a form of personal spiritual direction taking place in a public forum.

Preaching and the Tradition

SOME YEARS AGO I was fortunate to have the opportunity to live and study in the U.S. A major reason why I chose the U.S. was because I thought it would not be all that different from Australia. How wrong I was! I was amazed at the difference in attitude. I was astounded at how articulate and confident people were, particularly the children. Everyone seemed to know what they were about, and wanted to get on with it; and get on with it they did! The tenacity with which they attacked work and play never ceased to amaze me.

In seeing how the U.S. culture affected the way people reacted to life, I became more conscious of my own Australian cultural conditioning. My attitude to life was spiced with a good deal of "She'll be right, mate" and "We'll all be ruined!". We receive our cultural conditioning from the community in which we are immersed. It provides us with a framework that allows us to respond to life consistently and with meaning.

The Christian faith is really about immersing people in a *religious* culture. It is about giving people a framework for understanding and responding to life and its invitations. This Christian culture or world view has its origins in the life, death, and resurrection of Jesus. The historical Jesus, as the Way to the Father, showed us how to live as humans in a manner that will fulfill our human nature. Immediately after his death, the first disciples realized that to live in this way they would need the support of one another. It was this shared common interest in Jesus and the way he lived that brought them together and melded them into the first Christian community. Within this experience they recognized the presence of the Spirit. They came to realize that the community was the source of their enthusiasm and empowerment. It shaped their attitudes and responses to life. As well, it became their protection against personal bias when interpreting the presence of the Spirit in their lives, and soon became the legitimate protector of the integrity of the Christian message.

The Christian community has preserved these twofold responsibilities of enculturation and authentication over the centuries. In examining any ministry then, it is necessary to consider how the community has understood it at various times. Rather than try to provide a history of the ministry of preaching, I would like to look in some detail at how it is understood in the Acts of the Apostles and then how it is viewed by the Second Vatican Council. In examining these community documents, our interest is to see how they may help us to better understand and carry out the ministry of preaching in our own local churches.

In an excellent chapter in *A New Look at Preaching*, Raymond Brown examines the sermons in Acts. I would simply like to summarize some of the points he makes and add some personal observations. What will become clear is that Acts confirms many of the points already made in the previous chapters.

Brown begins by stating that while the sermons may have been put into the mouths of Stephen or Peter or Paul, they are the words of the author of Acts, written around A.D.80. That point made, Brown notes the diversity in the attitudes and theologies of the various preachers. This can arise from the background of the preacher. On the one hand, Peter, a Palestinian Jew, sees the Temple as an appropriate place for worship and it is the setting for a number of his homilies (3,1; 5,12). On the other hand, Stephen, a Hellenist, or a Jew from the Diaspora, obviously was critical of the Temple. He was accused of "making speeches against this holy place"(6,14). Both, however, are deeply committed to Christ. And both deliver telling homilies!

This diversity among the preachers in Acts reiterates the point made earlier that the fullness of the Christian message is far beyond the perception of any individual person or theology. *There is no one way to preach the gospel.* The more windows we have into the mystery that was revealed in Christ, the more comprehensive will become our understanding of what it means to be human. A variety of preachers within a community, with their own personal faith perceptions and theologies, are, if not essential, at least a tremendous advantage.

There is diversity too within the sermons themselves. Paul in Ch. 13 when addressing the "men of Israel", prefaces his sermon with a history of the Jewish people. In repeating the same proclamation to the "men of Athens" in Ch. 17, he changes the preface to a "Lord of heaven and earth" theme.

Respecting and responding to various audiences provides the preacher in the local church with some challenges and a good deal of hard work. All would be familiar with the way in which audiences alter at the various Sunday assemblies. The 6 p.m. Saturday congregation is usually very different from that at 7 a.m. on Sunday. These differences need to be respected if we are to preach effectively.

While stationed in a small country parish, I was amazed at the difference between people at two of the Mass centers. One group were in the main wheat farmers, whereas the other group were sheep graziers. Their attitude to the land was different; when one group wanted rain often the other wanted fine weather; their economic interests varied according to their market interests. The difference in the congregations often required a different preface if not a different homily!

According to Brown, the main theme running throughout the sermons in Acts is the proclamation of what God has done for us in Christ. As has been said, Jesus, through his birth, life, death, and resurrection, revealed a new way of being human. He is the authentic Word of God, and it is this Word that is to be, for the Christian, the authentic interpreting tool of their experience. Being Christian does not simply mean behaving in a particular way. It also involves the explicit interpretation of this behavior, according to the Word revealed in Christ. This "naming" is integral to Christian identity.

This aspect of the sermons charges the preacher with the responsibility of helping people interpret their experience specifically in the light of the birth, life, death and resurrection of Jesus. This Christ dimension is at the heart of the ministry. It demands of the preacher to be able to theologize rather than simply present theology. The minister is called to bring into dynamic interaction the experience of the listener with the revelation of Christ. Such an emphasis will guard against any psychologizing or individualizing of the gospel message.

Acts 2,37f. gives some clear guidelines to the expected result of good preaching. As a result of Peter's first sermon, we are told that

21

the listeners were "cut to the heart" and asked "What must we do?" In reply, Peter told them, "You must repent, and every one of you must be baptized in the name of Jesus Christ for the forgiveness of your sins and you will receive the gift of the Holy Spirit . . ."

Peter's preaching obviously impacted strongly upon the lives of his listeners. His homily was not simply an interesting dissertation upon a man who had recently gained headlines in the local community. Rather, his intention was to encourage people to change, and to change *now*.

The aim of preaching today is the same. It is an impact ministry that sets out to elicit from its hearers a response that will result in changed behavior. While preaching will sometimes be directed at reassuring and consoling people, it is primarily a disturbing ministry that will often require of the minister a good deal of courage.

Brown makes the excellent point that the ministry calls all to conversion. Many of us who have lived within the Christian tradition for the majority of our lives can tend to think of conversion as something that is really only for the hardened sinner. Our catechetical tradition can tend to lull us into thinking we really do know what God expects of us and, at most, we only need a little touch up here and there. But it is from this world of complacency that many of us need liberation. Indeed, as has been true in the past, those who may need conversion most can be those who appear to be living within the Christian tradition. Jolting people out of their complacency may well be one of the major goals of contemporary preaching.

Preaching is to lead to baptism. While Jesus himself was not a "baptizer", the first Christian communities quickly adopted the practice of baptism as the visible sign or sacrament of entry into the community. The Christian life can only be lived from within a true and faithful community. If any personal conversion is to endure, the convert will quickly need the support and encouragement of people who view life in the same way. Preaching aims at facilitating development of the community by encouraging people to live the community life to the full. This goal constitutes a great challenge in a world obsessed with the individual. Much of our preaching today has fallen prey to this obsession, and has tended to stress individual conversion. Modern preachers need to be aware that to be Christian alone is a contradiction in terms.

Acts spells out some of the benefits to those who respond to the invitations of good preaching. They will "experience a forgiveness of their sins" and "receive the gift of the Holy Spirit"(2,38). When we live in a way which is less than we were created to live, we experience sin. An important aspect of the ministry of preaching is to draw our attention to these destructive attitudes and behaviors at work within ourselves and within our communities. It encourages us to own them and to recognize them as alienating us from who we truly are, and are called to be. The ministry does this within the positive revelation made known in Jesus. It alerts us to the indwelling Spirit already and always present within us, and urges us to respond to the invitations of this Spirit, found at the heart of our ordinary human experience. In this way, we are gradually reconciled with ourselves: our sins are forgiven. At the same time, we come to appreciate the graciousness of life itself and the Spirit that is the source of this graciousness. Indeed, good preaching does help people "receive the gift of the Holy Spirit"

Finally, in Acts we see the message of Christ translated into a new idiom. The first preachers did not have precedents. They were spurred on by their own personal experience of the Spirit and wished to share this with others. Their primary aim was to share the experience so that others could know the freedom they themselves had come to know and live out of.

Maybe there is too much "looking over the shoulder" in our preaching today. Maybe we are so concerned with being faithful to past presentations of the Christian message that we have lost sight of the Spirit alive in people and communities today. Just as the first preachers created the gospel for their own day and for their own communities, so too today's preachers need to be gospel creators.

The Second Vatican Council called the Catholic Christian tradition to a renewal of its liturgical practice. This included an examination of the role of the homily within the liturgical celebration. The Council called for a homiletical style similar to that used in the early Church. There, the homily was based upon the scripture text chosen for the celebration. Its aim was to help people understand their lives in the light of these texts and then to celebrate their shared faith in the Eucharist.

Over the centuries, the understanding and use of the homily or sermon changed, usually as a result of the cultural circumstances in which the Christian community found itself. For example, in the Middle Ages, the homily became a platform for the theological speeches of the scholastics. In so doing, it became separated from the remainder of the liturgical celebration. Significantly, the

23

pulpit was removed from the sanctuary. After the Reformation, within the Catholic tradition the sermon again became primarily a teaching ministry. It was by far the most effective way in which the hierarchy was able to teach the faithful the dogmatic and moral doctrine of Trent.

Little changed in the way the sermon was understood and used between the post-Reformation period and Vatican II. In the 1950's and early 1960's in Australia, the sermon was still used to teach doctrine. To this end it was not uncommon for a bishop to send out a syllabus specifying what was to be preached for the whole year. Usually these subjects bore no relationship to the scripture used in the liturgy.

Part of the genius or inspiration of the Council was its recognition that one of the effective ways to change attitudes is to change language. With regard to the ministry of preaching, it went a long way in helping people renew their understanding of the ministry by speaking about the ministry with a "new" language. While the Council documents do use "sermon", the preferred term is "homily". This word has its origins in the Greek *homileo*, which means "a familiar conversation". In choosing this word, the Council paved the way for a shift in our basic understanding of the homily. Rather than be seen as a formal teaching tool, the Council suggested the homily should be characterized by its familiarity, both in content and presentation. While preaching about doctrine is not precluded, the homily is seen more as a ministry of the heart, calling for personal and communal conversion, rather than a dissertation upon the "teachings of the church".

In its various documents, the Council presents us with guidelines for the practice of the ministry. The document on the Liturgy (35,52) and the subsequent Instruction for the Implementation of the Constitution on the Liturgy (53–55) both stress that the homily is an integral part of the liturgy of Eucharist. By helping people bring their lives to the gaze of the Scriptures, the homily prepares and disposes people to experience and celebrate in sacrament the presence of God in their lives.

Because most people find it difficult to maintain a high level of intensity for any length of time, liturgists, as well as our own experience, tell us that good liturgy needs to have a natural ebb and flow to it. It builds to a high point, only to relax before building to the next high point. The rhythm of the Eucharistic liturgy is built around three high points: the homily, as the conclusion of the liturgy of the Word; the doxology and great Amen, as the conclusion of the Eucharistic liturgy; and the communion as the conclusion of the fraction and sharing liturgy. While this liturgical rhythm is not just about time, it does provide us with a context in which to address the length of the homily. While it certainly is the high point of the liturgy of the Word, in terms of time, it must always remain a part of the whole liturgy. If in a 50-minute liturgy, the homily takes up 20 minutes, then there is every chance that it has disrupted the flow of the liturgy. In determining how long to speak, a good homilist will be alert to the rhythm of the liturgy of which this particular homily is a part. As well, of course, we must also realistically assess our capacity to hold an audience. While in most areas of our lives we underestimate ourselves, in this area it would seem that many preachers well and truly *over*estimate themselves.

In the document on Revelation, Art. 21, the Council suggests that "... all preaching of the Church must be nourished and ruled by Sacred Scripture". Art. 4 of the "Ministry and Life of Priests" reads, "If it is to influence the mind of the listener more fruitfully, such preaching must not present God's word in a general and abstract fashion only, but it must apply the perennial truths of the gospel to the concrete circumstances of life." This call to mediate the interaction between the scripture and the lived experience of people is the great challenge that the Council lays down to today's preachers.

To assist, the Church introduced into its Eucharistic liturgy a three-year cycle of readings. This allows people to be exposed to a good deal of both the Old and the New Testaments. The Christian message is carried by the whole gospel, and preachers need to resist the temptation to shy away from the more difficult texts.

In Art. 19 of the Decree on "Priestly Formation", the Council calls for seminarians to be "carefully instructed" in matters relating to a number of pastoral activities including preaching. After being involved in the training of future pastors for a number of years, I have become painfully aware of the inadequacies of the present seminary system as a means of training people for effective presbyteral ministry.

The entrance requirements for seminaries today tend to stress personal integrity and intellectual competence. They place little emphasis upon the charismatic giftedness of people. Consequently, much time and effort goes into instructing people who, to put it bluntly, simply do not have the gift of preaching. They may well be people of great intellect and integrity, but if they cannot effectively preach, they should not be entrusted with the ministry.

The Council has stressed the importance of this ministry for the coming of the Kingdom. For its own good, it would seem that the local Christian community also needs to recognize the importance of the ministry and take a lot more care before it calls someone to it.

Clarifying
the Task

The Aim of Preaching

I HAVE HEARD many excellent homilies over the years. One was based on the story of the temptations of Jesus and it came just as the Allies were completing the bloody rout of Iraq from Kuwait. The preacher captured my attention by referring to the war and especially the might of the military power of the Allies. He went on to talk about our strengths, both communal and personal, and how easily they can become our Achilles heel. He then reflected upon the gospel story in terms of these sorts of experiences.

As I sat there, I thought of my own strengths and how often they had caused me problems. Somehow I resolved to become more aware of them with a view to appreciating rather than abusing them. As I left that church, I knew that, due to a good homily, a little of my inner self had been liberated. I also had a heightened awareness of what was happening in the war and of the need for the Allies to avoid any abuse of power.

All of the good homilies I have heard have shared two common characteristics. Firstly, during the homily I have become aware of God's presence in my life. Each of them became a vehicle for an actual experience of God. Sometimes this experience was passing; on a couple of occasions it was quite profound. Secondly, each of the homilies has, one way or another, called me to change. Some called me to change through making me aware of the graciousness of God present in my life; some by drawing my attention to the destructive patterns at work in my life; but all have called me to change.

My experience with good homilies, which I am sure I share with many, simply supports what I believe Scripture and tradition suggest should be the aim of the ministry of preaching. Good preaching seeks:

a. to dispose people to experience God during the liturgy;
b. to invite people to conversion, to a change of heart.

Let us examine each of these aims individually.

A. The Homily Aims at an Experience of God

As we have seen, the homily is an integral part of the Eucharistic liturgy and as such, shares the same goal. The whole liturgy is designed to dispose people to actually experience the presence of God during the liturgy itself. The role of the homily is to tap the memories and dreams, hopes and needs of the gathered people and bring them to the light of the gospel. The personal and communal responses to the homily are then celebrated and affirmed in the sacramental Eucharist that follows.

SOME CHARACTERISTICS OF RELIGIOUS EXPERIENCE

Since the homily aims at facilitating an experience of God for people, understanding how they perceive God, and talk about that experience can be very beneficial to the preacher.

Let me begin by sharing a couple of my own experiences of God. They may help to trigger some of your memories which can be used to test the observations that we make about such experiences.

I remember well one Sunday morning not so long ago. It was one of those magical Sydney autumn days. I had been invited by friends to brunch and we had a delightful time together. Later I drove home along the harbor. The water was shimmering. As I drank in the beauty of the view, I had an overwhelming feeling of somehow being connected with Life itself. I can still remember exclaiming to myself, "God! Life is good!". How appropriate. For in that moment I knew the gracious love of God.

My father's funeral Mass was another significant occasion for me. For some reason I had always feared presiding at the funerals of my parents. As it has turned out, they have been two of the privileged moments of my life. At Dad's funeral I was particularly anxious. As I walked into the church and heard the music, deep down a strange peace came over me. As the Eucharist progressed I was filled with an absolute conviction that Dad lived and that despite the sadness all would be well.

When I tell these stories people tend to nod their heads. While some of the details may be different, the core of the experience is familiar territory for most. Such experiences are marked by a number of characteristics, some of which are important for the ministry of preaching.

They tend to "break in" upon us. They are a *gift* which invites us to respond. This first and most important characteristic of religious experience signals a warning to preachers. Conversion comes through God's liberating grace. While the manner in which the preaching ministry is exercised may substantially contribute to the conversion process, it can never initiate it. The best the homilist can do is *dispose* people to experience God.

It is also important to note that religious experiences tend to *invite* people to respond. The experience itself generates an enthusiasm that empowers people to carry out their response. Good homilies are also marked with an invitational tone calling forth an enthusiastic response, rather than an obligatory tone calling forth a guilt-based response.

Religious experiences are primarily relational. They disclose to us that we are in relationship with a God that grounds our whole life. Other than God's interest in us as individuals, little is disclosed of what He is like in Himself. This aspect of religious experience will be treated more fully when we take a closer look at conversion. However, it does suggest that homilies should be more concerned with our relationship with God rather than with discussing His nature.

What the preacher needs to realize most of all is that these experiences happen, more often than not, in the ordinariness of life. They come through loved ones and friends, forgiveness, sex, music, art, sport, thinking, travel, work. Indeed, any human experience is capable of mediating these experiences. Our world is God's dwelling place. It is by becoming more familiar with our world that we are more likely to encounter God. Homilies are not about removing people from the world in which they live; they are about helping them discover the presence of the Spirit within that world.

RELIGIOUS EXPERIENCE AND THE IMAGINATION
All transcendental experience has two complementary dimensions. There is, firstly, the finite human situation. In the examples I

have given this was the harbor and the funeral. But there is also the Mystery or "God" dimension. This is known in and through the finite situation. Both these apparently incompatible dimensions, the finite and the infinite, have to be held at the same time for the experience to maintain its integrity. To deny one or the other is to deny the whole. Without the harbor, there was no vehicle for the experience of Mystery; without the Mystery, the occasion would have been no different to many others when I have admired the beauty of the harbor but have not experienced God in the way I did that morning.

As well, religious experience tends to capture all of us. It has an intellectual component: we know God is with us. There is also an emotional component: often we well up with feelings during the experience. It even has a physical component: there is sometimes a muscle contraction, or a sensation down the back of our neck. Religious experience involves a way of knowing that is different from the way we know most other things, and requires some further consideration.

The facility within the human psyche that allows us to maintain the integrity of such experiences is the imagination. Many people think of the imagination as that power we have within our minds to escape from reality. They see it mainly in terms of fantasy. While the imagination may be used for fantasy, it is primarily the function of the psyche that we use to perceive those dimensions of life that go beyond the capacity of our intellect. Kathleen Fischer describes it as a prism: the imagination receives the white light of our ordinary experience, breaks it open and allows us to see the many colours contained in the light of that experience. Through it we know the indescribables of life: love, beauty, hope, fear. Most importantly, it is the imagination that allows us to *know* God's presence directly within our human experience.

Consequently, people's imaginations are the "happy hunting ground" of good preachers. To assist people to experience God during the homily, somehow the imaginations of people need to be activated. The preacher will need to stimulate people to look at their experience through their imaginations, in the hope they may perceive within that experience the presence of God. A good first step towards effective preaching is to be familiar with the language of the imagination and the characteristics of imaginative knowledge.

The nature of the imagination dictates its language. It is essentially metaphorical. In a metaphor, we use something with which we are familiar to describe something with which we are less familiar or even unfamiliar. It allows us to make new and different connections and associations. The imagination can use and respond to an *image* such as a family photo. It uses the image to "make present" the family members. Or it may use a *symbol* like a flag to speak of the identity of a nation. In this case there is no obvious resemblance between the symbol and the symbolized. They are "thrown together" (which is what the Greek *sum ballein* actually means), by the national heritage. In religious symbols, for example in the Christian Eucharist, a profane object, like bread or wine, is used to make present the divine, Christ.

The primary verbal language of the imagination is the *story*. Stories use word pictures to make present a previous lived situation or an imagined situation in order to communicate its meaning and significance. They introduce a personal dimension in their telling. Because of this they are among the most engaging and powerful forms of communication, and have a significant place in the ministry of preaching which we will examine in some detail presently.

When stories speak of the core meaning of life itself, they are referred to as *myths*. The Christian myth is told when we tell the story of the life, death and resurrection of Jesus. In the telling of that story, Christians believe they tell the story of every person.

The most comprehensive form of imaginative communication is through *ritual*. Rituals use images, symbols, stories and myths in a rhythmic, integrated way. Communities use ritual to enact the fundamental or core metaphor that gives people the framework out of which they are able to make meaning of their lives. For Christians this is Eucharist. In this ritual, Christians celebrate the life, death and resurrection of Jesus, and in so doing are able to look at their own lives in the light of his attitudes and values, and discover within those lives the liberating presence of the Spirit of God.

STORIES IN PREACHING
Within the ritual of Eucharist, and outside of it for that matter, preachers are probably best described as tellers of stories: they tell their own story of faith, either directly or indirectly; they tell the story of the particular community to which they minister; and they tell the story of the life, death and resurrection of Christ and the presence of his Spirit in our world. Story is the language used most

33

in the ministry of preaching and it warrants some more detailed examination.

To begin with, it is worth noting that there are two different types of stories. Some stories are used to illustrate a point, e.g. I wish to describe what I might think is true compassion and so I will tell of how Dorothy Day was prepared to share her bed with prostitutes from the street. Such stories draw on the imagination to bring feeling and depth to a conviction established by reason and intellect.

Other stories are told for their own sake. Often the tellers are still struggling with the significance of the experience and it is only in the retelling that they are able to discover the true meaning of what had happened to them. These stories have a different tone about them. They tend to be told from the inside, and with a good deal more feeling than stories used as examples.

Preachers can benefit from an appreciation of this distinction. Both styles of storytelling are very powerful. If preachers use stories as examples, they will need to be careful not to use this powerful tool to impose on their listeners their own ways of thinking and experiencing God. Stories told for their inherent meaning are much more invitational in tone. They are simply shared without extensive interpretation beyond maybe a comment about what the significance of the story was for the teller.

I like to think of a preacher as an impressionist painter. An impressionist painting has a soft focus in contrast to the hard focus of more traditional styles. While the painter's interpretation of the scene is obvious, the viewer is also invited to become involved in the interpretation of the painting. Preachers will be most helpful if they simply offer the images and stories to their listeners and allow them to make their own specific connections. When we deal with the structure of the homily, I will attempt to show how this use of story can be a most effective component.

STORYTELLING IN PREACHING

Telling stories is an art, but one that most can master with practice. The power of the story will depend to a degree on the way it is told. Here are a few guidelines I have found helpful.

I have found that the stories that have made a deep impression on people are those I personally have also found powerful. I would suggest then that we should choose the stories we use carefully. The ones whose power we ourselves have experienced will probably work best. We must be careful, however, not to impose our own interpretation as the only possible one. The stories' own integrity must be respected. This is true whether they are from our own experience or fictional.

In preparation, get to know the story well. Memorize the key words and phrases that carry the real power and feeling. Unless you are absolutely familiar with it, you will have to give too much attention to the details and the power of the telling will suffer.

In telling the story, tell it from within the story itself. Try to imagine in your mind's eye what you are telling. Initially, you will probably find yourself looking at the experience and recounting what you see. As you become more familiar with it you will find that you begin to enter the story and feel with the people in it. These feelings are translated by the tone of your voice. By telling it aloud a few times, you will gradually begin to grasp its natural rhythm.

When you tell the story to a group, you will soon become aware of the way in which it engages them. In the telling of the story, a good storyteller becomes transparent. People become so involved in the story that they forget the storyteller. Storytelling is an art which needs to be practiced but, with good preparation I believe most are able to become competent.

As storytellers, preachers need to use an abundance of word pictures that resonate with their listeners and the gospel. The masters of this type of language are novelists and movie makers, artists and musicians. Preachers have a great need to stimulate their own imaginations so as to constantly add to the images they are able to call upon. A few hours a week reading a good novel or a visit to a movie can prove invaluable for good preaching.

THE TRUTH OF THE IMAGINATION

While it is the whole person that knows, and there are risks in oversimplifying the knowing process, the imaginative knowing process, and the truths known from this process, do have some distinctive characteristics.

The imagination always deals with the specific: specific sense experience, specific concepts. It is interested in and notices *this* tree, *this* idea, rather than trees and ideas. Having received the specific image, it then breaks it apart and allows us to see the "more than meets the eye" dimensions of the experience.

Preachers take note! *Specific* images and stories are the most effective way of stimulating the imaginations of listeners. While the imagination can deal with general concepts, it does not grasp them as quickly nor as enthusiastically.

Imaginative knowing is much more lateral than the knowledge of reason. It involves the whole person by introducing feeling, emotion and will into the knowing process. This does not exclude reason. On the contrary, reason and intelligence are the guiderails that prevent the imagination from spinning off into fantasy. However, the imaginative process will not submit itself to the narrow constraints of rational truth. Indeed, if we try to subject it to the criteria of rational truth it simply withdraws.

By introducing these feelings, the imagination provides energy to the psyche, empowering it to exercise the will and act. A great example of the power of imaginative language is the story of Cicero and Diosthenes. Cicero spoke and people exclaimed, "What a great oration!". Diosthenes spoke and people exclaimed, "Let's march!". One knew the language of reason and the other the language of the imagination.

The feeling character of imaginative knowledge and language is very obvious. Rather than possessing imaginative knowledge, we tend to dwell within it. Imaginative truth has a way of gently inviting us to surrender to it. Consequently, when speaking out of the imagination we will speak with all the feelings and conviction of what that truth means for us.

Good preachers will respect the gentleness of imaginative truth by inviting people to participate in the truth rather than trying to force it upon them. They will also be aware that imaginative communication depends as much upon the listener as it does upon the person who is speaking. Should the listeners refuse to engage themselves in what is being said, there is very little the preacher can do. Even the Word of God has difficulty in taking root in a hardened heart. Like all ministries, there is a mutuality in the ministry of preaching that is essential for its effectiveness.

B. The Homily Aims at Personal and Communal Conversion

From the first homily given by Peter in Acts, preaching has always aimed at touching people's hearts. It has always been about conversion; about helping people make changes in their lives so that they might fulfill their human potential by living according to the Spirit. As the result of Jesus' preaching, people changed (Lk. 7,18–23); as the result of Peter's preaching, people changed (Acts, 2,37); and as the result of preaching today, people should change. It is both as simple and as difficult as that!

What clues does a contemporary understanding of the process of conversion have for today's preacher?

CONVERSION AND THE KNOWING PROCESS

Bernard Lonergan provides us with some valuable insights that help us understand the conversion process. Conversion involves coming to know God in a new way. According to Lonergan, in the process of knowing, the human psyche is constantly involved in one of four operations:

      Experiencing

      Understanding

      Judging

      Deciding

First we *experience* something (a view, food, friendship, God). We then try to *understand* what this experience means for us. Once we have understood it, we then *judge* it. We determine whether we find it important or trivial, fascinating or boring. Finally, we *decide* whether we want to have more of the experience or less of it. We will then act to either consolidate it or undermine it.

For the most part we are not explicitly conscious of these functions. They operate automatically as we move from one experience to another and to a large degree we remain personally detached from our experiences. There are occasions, however, when we do become explicitly aware of one or other of the functions. A particularly striking experience will cause us to investigate it and struggle to determine its significance. We will become conscious of the implications of the experience and have to decide how we are going to handle it.

The homilist is attempting to dispose people towards becoming conscious of these processes, especially in terms of transcendental experience. Think of a homily that has influenced you. Did it not make you aware of some previous experience, behavior or attitude? If so there is every chance it challenged you to examine the behavior or attitude and re-evaluate it according to the gospel. Finally, it probably left you with a decision to make about future behavior.

TRIGGER EXPERIENCES

The most difficult task for the homilist is to entice people to engage themselves explicitly in this process. We have seen how the languages of the imagination can assist in this task of triggering the memories of people. But the *sorts* of memories triggered are also important. In the process of conversion, some memories are more appropriate than others.

Within common human experience there are a number of "yearnings of the heart" that seek fulfillment. Every person seeks to love and be loved. We have a need to share with another in a way that we are able to reveal our innermost hopes and fears, knowing that the other will not destroy us in our vulnerability. As well, we have a need to be entrusted with the experiences and emotions of another. There is a desire in each of us to be given the opportunity to realize all kinds of potentialities that we feel within ourselves. We wish to make our contribution to the world and leave some kind of legacy behind us.

When a homilist can trigger memories that tap these needs, it usually happens that listeners are brought to a state of explicit consciousness. They will begin to re-examine their experience and possibly re-evaluate it in the light of the gospel. In achieving this the homily has played its part in the conversion process.

While religious experience can be had through any human experience, there are certain circumstances that carry religious experience more often than others. Special occasions dispose people to reflect upon their whole life: the birth of a child; the death of a spouse or parent; a family wedding; a stay in hospital; being near to a serious accident. In the reflection people often become aware of a transcendent presence grounding their lives. Times of utter devastation are also often times when people experience God. Stories told in Alcoholics Anonymous are a powerful example of how people find God in the midst of personal devastation. Similarly, times of shared vulnerability are also occasions of religious experience.

By telling stories of these types of experiences, the homilist is likely to trigger the interest of people and help them to consciously engage the functions of the psyche.

Then there are people's stories of conversion. We have already seen the power of story generally. It has no more powerful expression than when it is used to tell of someone's experience of God. These accounts can take a number of different forms. They may be stories about personal conversion in which there is a radical shift in the way people live. Like the occasion early this century when a newspaper reported the death of the wrong man. As a result, that person had the opportunity to read his own obituary. He was the inventor of dynamite and had made a fortune from its sale, especially for weapons of destruction. The newspaper described him as "the merchant of death". This was his moment of conversion. From then on he devoted himself to working for peace. He contributed huge sums of money for research that would contribute to the betterment of humankind. And he left a legacy that today is recognized worldwide. The man of course was Alfred Nobel, the instigator of the Nobel Prize.

Then there are stories of conversion in which faith is deepened. Like the story of Mother Teresa, who was so struck by the poverty she saw when visiting Bombay that she felt compelled to leave the security of her convent and go into the streets to care for the destitute and dying.

Finally, there are stories that tell of how people have lived as the result of their conversion experiences. Like a couple I know in Brisbane who decided to give up their comfortable lifestyle to work for the homeless men and women of the city. The love and compassion they showed towards the homeless was an inspiration not only to the homeless but to anyone who had the privilege to know them.

Again, these types of stories are likely to stimulate the interest of people, causing them to reflect upon similar experiences of their own.

THE VARIOUS AREAS OF CONVERSION

Conversion is an extremely complex process through which there is a transformation in the way we experience ourselves, others, the world and the universe. As well as the experiential dimension treated above, Lonergan suggests there are a number of different areas within a human person in which conversion takes place. He suggests that conversion may be religious, Christian, ecclesial, moral or intellectual. He makes these distinctions simply for the purpose of analysis and in no way does he infer that each of these aspects of humanness is separated from the others. In individuals, conversion tends to ebb and flow into all areas of a their lives. Let us look briefly at what Lonergan understands by each of these distinctions and how they may help the preacher.

Religious conversion comes about when a person becomes aware of what Rahner calls the "holy mystery" of life. Through a variety of transcendental experiences, people tend to grow in an awareness that all human life, and indeed all of creation, is grounded in the Transcendent. What is more, this Transcendent Mystery, called God, "breaks in" upon people in a most gracious way, disposing them to personalize their relationship with him. Once grounded in this conviction, a person is able to live life in hope and trust despite any personal human failure or suffering.

It can happen that people can be under the sway of this religious conversion and yet be at odds with the institutional churches. All of us would know people for whom this would be true. More significantly, in terms of preaching in worship, a person may be a participating church member and yet lack this religious conversion. As we have stressed, assisting people to appreciate the presence of the Spirit in ordinary human experience is a major aim of preaching.

Christian conversion is the recognition and acceptance that the life, death and resurrection of Jesus provides the fundamental paradigm for human living. The converted Christian sees Jesus as expressing in his incarnation the unconditional love of the Father for us. Jesus assured us that we no longer need to live in fear of God; that God's one desire is for us to fulfill our human potential. As well, Jesus provides us with the attitudes and values which will allow us to respond best to the Father's love.

Christian conversion involves a personal appropriation of the paschal mystery. Through the ages, the gospel text has been a primary vehicle of the paschal mystery. Today in all traditions, but particularly in the Catholic tradition, there is a renewed thirst for an appreciation of the gospel text. People look to their preachers as one of the ways of addressing this need. By assisting people to enter the text creatively, the preacher is able to help them use the text to interpret their ordinary human experience.

Appreciating this need in a community will encourage a preacher to respect the integrity of the text. It will also help overcome any temptation to stray from preaching the gospel of Christ.

The third level of conversion that Lonergan refers to is *ecclesial conversion*. By this he means that inner movement which draws people into community. As we appropriate and begin to live out of our chosen value system, we tend to seek out others who share our attitudes and values. For Christians, this involves joining with others in order to hear the Word, break the bread and bless the cup. As well, it involves a growing awareness of the social and political dimensions of our faith. Justice becomes an integral value in the judging of our experience.

This area of conversion within the community can prove to be a great challenge to the preacher. Much of the preaching tradition has lacked a community dimension. It has tended to foster personal conversion and hoped for some sort of a flow-on into the community. This has left many who were struggling with ecclesial conversion disillusioned. Often too, preachers have spoken out of a narrow ecclesiological model with little understanding of the dynamics of group life. In respecting the ecclesial conversion needs of people within their communities, preachers need to realize that community life is an integral part of the humanizing process. As well, however, they need to be aware that there are many ways in which Christians can be in community. Offering community-oriented analysis of attitudes and behavior is integral to good Christian preaching.

Moral conversion involves the quest for authenticity. At this level people seek to do good simply because it *is* good. Their motivation is not governed by rewards or punishments, appearances or public opinion. They try to transcribe the values in their hearts into their behavior. It involves every personal and public thought and action where gospel values are at stake. It was the central quest in the lives of people like Thomas More and Martin Luther King.

Preachers may well respond to this level of conversion within their communities as much through attitude as through the content of their homilies. The preacher is on the same journey towards wholeness as those to whom he or she preaches. Preaching is as much a sharing with people as it is a leading or a challenging of people. To be able to somehow articulate the inner struggle for integrity and wholeness of individuals and the community is a marvelous gift which the preacher can offer.

The final level of conversion that Lonergan speaks of is *intellectual conversion*. This is the slow and often painful process through which the thinking person experiences liberation and integration of the mind. Through this conversion people become aware of, and respect, the complexity of life and its mysteries. They begin to realize that often things are not as they may appear to be on the surface. They realize the limitations of knowledge itself and of the fact that no one discipline can adequately describe all of creation.

While this is an extremely important area of conversion, it is one that is addressed better through a ministry of adult education than through the ministry of preaching. Having said this, it needs to be stressed that although they may not be articulated in the homily itself, sound philosophical and theological principles are always the basis of good preaching.

CONVERSION MEANS FALLING IN LOVE

Let me conclude our reflection upon conversion by taking a completely different view of the process. I was chatting with a friend one day when he suddenly paused and said, "You know I have always believed in Christ but I have never really fallen in love with him." What a profound observation!

Preaching aims to help people to fall in love with Christ.

"Falling in love" is a very accurate phrase, for that is what happens to us: we *fall* in love. Most relationships begin in a fairly low-key way. We meet someone and feel comfortable with them. We like the way they look and behave. We go out together a few times and find their company increasingly enjoyable. We find ourselves daydreaming about them and wanting to spend more and more time with them. They become the center of our world. We become immersed in a wonderful experience of powerful feelings and emotions. In love, we *fall*. We do not embark upon a number of reasoned, logical steps that will bring us to the love of another. Rather, we leap out of self towards the other, hoping and desiring that they will receive us in a relationship of mutual giving and receiving.

While such a leap involves the whole person, their intelligence, emotions and will, initially these individual functions are touched only intuitively and implicitly. We are caught up so much in the immediacy of the whole experience that there seems neither the space, the time, nor the need for the sort of reflection necessary to understand the roles of the various functions of the psyche. Our responses tend to be spontaneous, although obviously influenced unconsciously by our present value system and attitude to life. They are made from within the experience, and it is the experience itself which empowers us to live out the decisions we make.

Falling in love with another or with God, or both, is a passionate affair. To effectively minister in this area we need to be willing to enter into the passion of the experience. Our own personal relationship with God, the language we use in our homilies, the content we choose, all need to be shot through with passion. Being a midwife in this love affair between a person and God is one of the most exciting and fulfilling dimensions of the ministry of preaching.

Viewing the ministry of preaching in this way requires a substantial shift in understanding for the majority of preachers. It will also require a change in homiletical style.

The Mindset We Bring to Preparing a Homily

BY ESTABLISHING some concrete aims for the ministry of preaching, we end one search and begin another. It is helpful to see the preaching task in terms of facilitating for people an experience of God and then encouraging them in their individual journeys of faith. To have a clear and concrete goal always increases effectiveness. But as the result of establishing our aims, we are faced with developing a homiletical style capable of achieving them. For most, this will require a fundamental shift in their perception of the preaching task.

When we sit down to write a homily there are a number of unconscious filters that actually precondition the style of homily we produce. Previous chapters have tried to make us aware of some of these and sharpen our awareness of them. We saw how our lived theology of revelation can affect our preaching. If our theology is essentially deductive, we will tend to apply revealed truths to our present situation. If our theology is more inductive, we will be more concerned with discerning the Spirit present within human experience.

The chapter on the aims of preaching endeavored to address how we perceive the preaching task and suggested that the ministry has at least two concrete aims: to facilitate an experience of God and to encourage people in their conversion journeys.

There is however, one other significant factor which needs to be addressed before we can look more closely at developing an appropriate and effective homiletical style. And this is the language of our culture.

The fundamental symbol system that conditions how people

perceive experience is language. It provides us with the lenses that allow us to see and understand. It not only shapes *how* we see things, but also *what* we see. The power of language was well demonstrated in an experiment with an Indian tribe in North America. Their language had only three words to distinguish various colors: *lak* for red; *tit* for green–blue; and *talak* for yellow–orange–brown. The Indians could only perceive three colors; they were unable to distinguish color in the way English-speaking people can. Their language influenced both how they saw and what they saw.

The English language has its roots in the Graeco–Roman languages of the ancient world. These languages were "assembling" alphabetical languages. They put letters together to make words and they put nouns, phrases, clauses and verbs together to create sentences. They are languages with a strong conceptual bias. The Greeks mastered the art of abstraction and generalization and this was reflected in their language. In contrast to the Graeco–Roman languages, the Chinese language and its derivatives are much more visual. The symbols of those languages often *look like* what they are symbolizing.

English, having grown out of this Graeco–Roman tradition, shares both its strengths and weaknesses. One of the strengths is its capacity for definition and description. English has by far the greatest vocabulary of all modern languages and is constantly growing. As well, it has a built-in desire for clarity which makes it a "tight" language, demanding accuracy both in expression and understanding. As a consequence, it requires the speaker to be in "control" of the language.

One area in which the structure of the language has exercised a great deal of influence is in the processes of education. The way people are educated in the English-speaking world will be largely governed by ideas, concepts, reason and logic. They will be encouraged to have control over the content so that they are able to use it effectively. These are all characteristics that are carried within the structure of the language itself. Their influence is as great as it is, simply because they are part of the unconscious assumptions taken for granted in the educational process. It is just presumed that this is the best way to go about learning.

The educational philosophy used to teach most preachers theology bears all the marks of our cultural language. In my experience there is a strong bias towards abstract content in the theology courses presently offered in colleges concerned with ministry preparation. Students become capable of discussing theological principles and perspectives, but rarely develop the skills of being able to theologize in a pastoral setting. Theology, rather than theologizing, is taught.

This is not a direct criticism of the staff in such colleges. They are forced to teach within academic structures which support this more theoretical approach. Given different structures I am sure that the same staff could assist students to develop adequate theological skills. Nevertheless, this educational ideology develops within students a mindset unconsciously disposed towards the conceptual ordering of ideas in all forms of communication.

People taking courses on homiletics are not exempt from this ideology. Consequently, most bring this unconscious mindset to the homiletical task. They see the homily as a "mini-essay" in which the preacher is trying to communicate clearly an aspect of the Christian tradition. Such a mindset produces a particular homiletical style which has dominated Christian preaching for centuries.

In teaching courses in homiletics over the years, both to theological students and to pastors, I have found that it has been this mindset which has proved the major stumbling block to changing homiletical style. I have seen many who were convinced of the need to change as the result of an examination of the history and theory of the ministry. They were well motivated and very willing. However, they were so imbued with this ideological mindset of ordering ideas that they were frustrated in their efforts to change. It was only with a great deal of persistence and supportive criticism that they were able to free themselves so as to be able to choose their own style. Because it is unconscious, it is impossible to view the mindset directly. We can become aware of its presence and influence, however, through a number of characteristics obvious in homilies written under its sway.

Homilists working under the influence of this unconscious mindset will usually begin their preparation by trying to establish a clear and definite idea which they wish to communicate. This may come from some personal insight that their experience has triggered. More often than not it will come from the text, either as the text has impressed them or, and again more likely, as it has been interpreted by a commentator. They will try to clarify the idea in their own mind until they feel they understand it sufficiently to be able to express it clearly. Once this is clear and the homilist feels he or she is in control of the matter, then it remains to work out how to express it most convincingly. A foundation is laid that substantiates the idea. This may be done through a story or some kind of general statement of the theme. The idea is then presented as clearly and logically as possible. Again stories may be used, but they will be used as examples and illustrations of the idea being expressed. Its logical consequences will be drawn, usually with some kind of practical application.

The whole aim of the exercise is to convince the hearers of the validity of the idea, which will provide them with a new understanding out of which they will be able to live more fully the Christian life. As you can see it is a process marked by reason, logic and understanding.

In certain circumstances this homiletical style can be most effective. It has its own demands that require a good deal of preparation on the part of preachers. It is essential that they have clarified their own ideas. How often have we had to put up with preachers who in effect do their thinking aloud in the pulpit, jumping from one insight to another? While the preacher may feel he or she is gaining insight and inspiration from the exercise, the listener is usually planning the remainder of Sunday!

In this homiletical style, language is also important. The ideas and concepts need to be expressed in a way that is intelligible to the listener. Regardless of style, every homilist needs to remember that it is not what is said that is important in a homily so much as what is heard.

People will usually respond positively to the use of this didactic style of preaching. There are a number of reasons for this. Most Christians, like most preachers, have been given to understand that the ministry of preaching is about communicating the *truths* of the faith. Since they too have been under the sway of the pedagogical mindset we have described, it stands to reason they will believe these to be best communicated through a clear and logical conceptual presentation. Most of their experience of homilies will support these assumptions. Both preachers and listeners, then, are influenced and conditioned by a similar set of unconscious criteria which supports and makes acceptable this particular homiletical style.

I believe that this method has made a substantial contribution to the faith life of the community over the centuries, and will continue to be appropriate in certain circumstances. It has however, also severely restricted and inhibited the scope and effectiveness of the ministry of preaching. Much of the negative effect of this particular homiletical style has simply come through preachers becoming slaves to it. They neither knew, nor felt the need to know, any other style.

From our consideration of the history and tradition of the ministry within the Christian community, we have seen that preaching involves much more than the communication of ideas. It is about experience of God and conversion. A homiletical style that is basically about communicating ideas will be restricted in its ability to achieve these aims.

While understanding does play a significant role in faith and conversion, it is limited in its capacity to initiate and motivate the conversion process. This is why people tend to leave the homily in the church on Sunday, rather than live out its message throughout their week. While the preacher may have prepared well and the listener been willing to hear, the style or vehicle used is unable to facilitate an experience of God that motivates the person to live differently. So, people tend to say, "That was a great homily!" rather than, "Let's do this!".

This criticism challenges us to discover new ways in which the ministry may better achieve its aims and goals. I believe the mindset and dynamics that ground the language of *story* offer a new approach to preaching that assists in developing a homiletical style consistent with the aims of the ministry contained in its history and tradition.

Could I ask you to begin our considerations by reading this story? Read it slowly, allowing your imagination full play. If you can, read it out aloud, for this story is best told rather than read.

I have a friend who is a pastor in an inner city suburb here in Sydney. Like many inner city parishes, there are a good number of poor whose homes are the streets and parks. Often my friend had callers asking for money or food. He is a compassionate man, but time and experience had brought forth within him a cynical streak. He cared for the poor but was not going to be conned by them!

One winter's night, as he was about to watch the news, the doorbell rang. He opened the door and standing on his front step was a bag-lady. There are a number of these people in Sydney. They carry all their possessions with them in carry bags. My friend did not know the lady but there was something about her, so he invited her to come in out of the cold and sit down. He offered her a cup of tea and she thanked him but said she hadn't come to ask for anything. He was taken aback, for usually these people were after something. In fact she said: "I have come to *give* you something; two things really. First I want to tell you a story." My friend asked her to continue.

"A long, long time ago, before I was alive and before my mother was alive, there was a small village. It was much the same as most other villages except that in the center of the village square there was a table and on the table there was a loaf of bread. It had been there for as long as anyone could remember. No one ever touched the bread for there were all sorts of stories about what would happen if someone took it. Some of the stories said you would become a slave, others that you would be exiled, while still others said that you would die.

"The bread had become so important to the village that when a child turned sixteen their parents would bring them before the village elders and the elders would ask them if they wished to take the village bread. Of course, with all the stories, the young people quickly refused. Until one day, when a lad was brought by his parents to the table, and one of the elders asked him if he wished to take the bread. To the amazement of all he said 'Yes!' His parents were shattered. The elder asked them if they had told the boy all the stories and they assured him that they had. Still, they took the boy aside and told him the stories again. He came back and the elder asked him for the second time if he wished to take the bread and again he said 'Yes'. Never having been confronted with this before, the elder pleadingly asked the boy a third time. And again the boy said 'Yes'. And so the elder took the bread from the table and gave it to the boy.

"There was a strange feeling in the village that afternoon. People were expecting things to happen to the boy who had broken with the village tradition. But nothing happened. Over the following days and weeks the villagers began to notice a change in the boy. He began helping people in all sorts of ways. And in a sense he became a slave, but without becoming servile. What he did he did freely, and people were impressed by his compassion and care.

"After a few months the boy left the village and visited some of the neighboring villages and so I suppose you could say that he was exiled. Stories began to flow back to his village about the way he was encouraging people to care for one another. He was establishing himself as something of a prophet and people spoke highly of him wherever he went. He seemed to fill people with hope and freedom.

"After some time he returned to his own village. The elders had heard all that people said about him and became jealous. They began to remember how the village used to be when they had the table and the loaf. Since then things had changed and people were living differently. They cared for each other more and were not so dependent upon the elders for guidance and direction. In their collective wisdom, the elders decided that for the good of the village it would be best if this boy were done away with. And so they took him outside the village one night and put him to death."

My friend was intrigued by the story. The old lady looked at him and simply said, "Father, what would life be like if no one ever took the bread!"

With that she stood up and went out the door.

My friend was still sitting contemplating the story when he noticed that the lady had left one of her bags. He picked it up and went to the door but she was nowhere to be seen. He walked back inside and looked in the bag. For reasons he could only guess at, he put his hand in the bag and took out the top parcel. The paper unrolled and he saw that it was a loaf of bread. And he realized that he had taken the bread. He remembered then that the old lady had told him that she wished to give him two gifts. The story was the first; the loaf was the second.

He stood there dumbfounded. All sorts of thoughts from the story went through his mind: of slavery and exile and even death. But the thought that rose above all others was the last thing the lady said, "What would life be like if no one ever took the bread!" And he was filled with a Spirit of hope and enthusiasm!

This has always been a powerful story for me. When I have told it for others, they too have commented upon its power. What I would like to do presently, however, is not look at the content so much as at how the story actually *engages* us in its telling or reading. I would invite you to step back and reflect upon yourself as you read the story. Of course, the observations I am about to make apply to all stories regardless of whether the medium is an oral story, a movie, a play or a novel. If this story has not engaged you, then remember a novel or movie or play that did.

As the story begins we are usually an uninvolved observer. Often our attention is divided between it and a number of other concerns we might have. I suppose this is most obvious when we go to the movies. While we are watching the beginning of the movie, there are often a thousand and one other thoughts on our mind. When we listen to a story being told, at this stage our attention is usually as much on the teller as on the story.

As it begins to unfold there is a shift in our focus. The story gradually snares us, as it were, and we become an involved participant. We begin to relate to the characters and feel with them as they struggle and rejoice in the circumstances in which they find themselves. Our attention moves away from the teller and our world becomes the world of the story.

If the story "connects" with some of our deeper feelings and attitudes, it can happen that it allows us to view life from a different point of view. This is so often the case with good novels and drama. They transport us outside of ourselves in order for us to be able to see our lives differently. They do it with such feeling that they energize and encourage us to live according to the insights they may have disclosed.

We have all experienced this power of story: of how it can move us from one point of view to another. In modern times there has been no better example of how stories can change people's lives than in Alcoholics Anonymous. That fellowship began when two men found that through sharing their stories with others they were empowered to change attitudes sufficiently to be able to break the addiction of alcohol. Millions have had the same experience in the last 60 years.

The Judeao–Christian tradition has always known the power of story to call people to conversion. The Old Testament abounds with such stories. There is none better than that of David and Nathan in 2 Sam. 11–12. In that account Nathan himself uses a story to call David to conversion. When we read the line "You are the man", most of us can feel its sting in our own lives.

The master storyteller of course was Jesus himself. He used parables or stories to call people to conversion. He knew the power of story to communicate the message that he had for humankind. In the gospels so often we find him replying to a question by telling a story. In Lk. 10,25–37, the lawyer asks, "Who is my neighbor?" and Jesus replies with the story of the good Samaritan. In Lk. 15, the Pharisees and Scribes were complaining about him mixing with tax collectors and sinners and he replied with the story of the two sons. It is worth comparing the power of this *story* of love with the more conceptual treatment of love by Paul in 1 Cor. 13. It was through stories that Jesus expressed his understanding of human life and invited people into his world.

One of the vibrant ministries in the Catholic tradition is the Rite for the Christian Initiation of Adults. The initial guidelines for this rite stressed the importance of story in the process. Both the catechists and the candidates were encouraged to tell their stories of faith. If the candidates found the faith story of the catechists appealing, they were to be invited to learn a little more of the Christian story. Eventually, they would be invited to join a Christian community through Baptism.

Unfortunately, it has happened that much of the storytelling seems to have been lost in an obsession with communicating doctrine. If this ministry is to maintain its vibrance, I believe it will need to quickly recover its personal and communal storytelling, and depend less upon professionally produced catechetical programs, for it is in story that conversion of the heart takes place.

It is clear then that stories have a dynamic that gives them the capacity to help people experience life differently. This same dynamic allows stories not only to disclose but also to empower. Since the aim of preaching is to help people view life differently, and then live out of that new insight, any homiletical style that can utilize the dynamics of story should prove very effective.

The language of story achieves its power because of a number of structural dynamics. I would like now to describe some of these and show how they may assist us in the development of a new homiletical style. The following more general observations will be complemented by a later chapter in which I will use the dynamics to prepare a sample homily.

Just as a person intent upon communicating ideas brings a particular mindset to the task, so does the storyteller. From what has already been said, it is probably clear that since our linguistic and cultural conditioning supports a mindset disposed towards the communication of ideas, the development of a storytelling mindset will require us to put in place a number of conscious criteria that will keep us within the storytelling mode.

Storytelling is first and foremost an exercise in listening. As compared to the communication of ideas, where the writer tends to organize and control the content, storytellers tend to listen to the story and respond to what they hear. They feel with the content, and rather than control and organize their matter, storytellers endeavor to *shape* it in the way a sculptor might shape a statue. And like the sculptor, they are aware that the matter itself has much to contribute to the whole process. Often novelists will speak of how the characters in their novels have a life of their own, and how they contribute to the outcome of the story, at times almost independently of the novelist.

For homilists seeking a storytelling style, this most fundamental attitude is crucial from the beginning of the preparation process. In attending the various sources of the content of the homily, namely the text, the life of the community and their own life, it is important that they be prepared to listen to each of these "from the inside". They need to be more intent on hearing what is being said than trying to place order upon what they are hearing. How to do this will be treated when we look at each of these sources individually.

This listening attitude extends also to the composition of the homily. Whereas in the communication of ideas it is important to complete one point before moving on to the next, this is not true of storytelling. Stories tend to move in a more linear way, with one observation leading to another. Each stage of the story is open-ended. Often it leaves readers with a question in their mind as to where the story may go from here. The various observations made simply mark a path for the listener to walk along with the storyteller. In listening to the developing story of their homily, and responding to what they hear from within the process, it will often happen that the homily actually produced will be very different from that which the homilist had in mind at the beginning of the writing.

Stories are always set in space and time. It is the concreteness of the setting that contributes to the energy of the story. Within the particular setting, the characters have to struggle with life. If the setting is too broad, then everything seems too easy and the story becomes shallow and loses power.

The movie *Dances with Wolves* is a good example of the important contribution which constraints of time and place make to the energy and power of a story. It is a simple plot. A cavalry officer is sent to a remote post just after the American Civil War. The sheer isolation of the place forces him to reach out to the Indian tribe that inhabits the land. In a very powerful way the film tells of how he befriends and is befriended by the tribe. This is a stormy process and the story draws its power from the respect the storyteller has for this storminess, brought on by the wariness of both the white man and the Indians. Had the storyteller opted to remove the constraints, thus making the task easy for the characters, no doubt the story would have lost its power.

In terms of homilies, the constraints of time and space are dictated by the lived experience of the listening community. An effective homilist will need to be able to convey to his listeners a real understanding of the true situations of their lives and the life of the community. It is within these situations that people are seeking the light and guidance of the gospel. A homily offering solutions to the general problems of humankind has little or no value. To announce bland "gospel solutions" to human problems without first experiencing and feeling the problem at depth is to disregard the constraints of time and space. Homilies that wish to use the dynamics of story will always need to remain in the concrete, both in terms of the content they deal with, and the manner in which it is expressed.

The genius of the great novelists, playwrights and movie makers is to be able to fashion their stories within the limitations of concrete settings in time and space in such a way that listeners are able to make their own general abstractions from the stories. Again *Dances with Wolves* is a good example. As the characters struggle with feelings familiar to us, our own perception of what is important in life is brought into focus. While not a word is spoken about the concepts of love or compassion or prejudice in the movie, few would walk away without asking a number of serious questions about each of these areas of their lives. In identifying with the characters and their struggles, we are able to recognize our own struggles. Often the characters can lead us along paths previously unknown.

Like stories, homilies are about sharpening the listeners' perceptions of life as it is lived. To be fully alive is to be involved in a web of relationships and experiences that are ever changing. These are the sources of our most profound feelings of joy and fulfillment. They are also the wellsprings of great confusion and turmoil. Life is a struggle; but a struggle necessary for us to fulfill our human potential. Just as the characters of a story allow listeners to experience their own personal struggles, so must the homily. Communities need to perceive that their preachers are aware that life is not black and white and that any number of considerations may cloud a particular issue. As well, they need to be given the opportunity to feel their own struggles during the homily without judgment or premature solutions. If this can be achieved, there is every chance that as the homily progresses the listener may well be led along new and liberating paths.

Central to every story is its plot. This is the path along which the listeners are led by the writer. The structure of the plot is what gives a story the power to initially engage listeners, and then maintain their interest. It is from the structure that the story draws its suspense.

A typical plot usually begins with the writer painting a scenario that involves some conflict, ambiguity or discrepancy. For the story to engage the listeners, this scenario needs to be real for them. While there are any number of ways in which this may be done, it will often involve either a lived situation of the listeners or one that is easily envisaged.

The writer then adds to the discrepancy or the ambiguity by introducing new and often unexpected details. This may be done through interaction between the characters or through development within the characters themselves. The listener is encouraged to look for some sort of resolution to the dilemma that has been painted. While heightening the ambiguity, the writer usually includes some clues as to how it will be resolved. In most good stories the actual resolution comes in some sort of reversal. The unexpected happens. The story is then brought to an appropriate conclusion.

Again let us use *Dances with Wolves* as an example. The writer, particularly through the cinematography, paints a picture of total isolation. Immediately the question arises "How will the officer survive?" Discrepancy has been achieved. As the movie progresses, different factors are introduced until the officer goes to find the Indian tribe and on the way comes across an injured Indian woman whom he picks up and returns to the tribe. This initiates a whole new set of ambiguous circumstances. Eventually, he falls in love with the woman and chooses to live with the tribe despite the threats and beatings of the cavalry. The real twist comes when it is discovered that the woman was not an Indian but had been raised by them after her parents had been killed during a raid in her childhood. The movie ends with the two white people riding away from the tribe in order to protect the tribe from the wrath of the cavalry who are now hunting the officer for treason.

It is a simple but beautifully crafted plot that remains faithful to the principles and dynamics of good storytelling. As a result it holds the audience's attention for most of the three hour running time.

While we will look at this structure in more detail in a later chapter, a couple of observations are relevant here. It is important that the homilist begins by painting a discrepancy that is *real* to the listener. In order to engage people, they need to feel there is something at stake. This is not to suggest that preachers are restricted to merely to speaking about what people want to hear. Indeed, as we saw when looking at the role of characters in story, much of the power of story is caught up in its ability to allow people to "overhear" their own perceptions through the characters. A good homilist is able to paint a discrepancy that will allow people to "overhear" their own situations, even though they may be reluctant to admit or address them.

People will only allow themselves to be led through a plot if they trust the writer to provide them with some sort of resolution. If we buy a novel by a particular author and find that he is unable to provide a tenable resolution to any discrepancies he may have created, there is every chance we will not buy that author again. Much the same is true of homilies. Homilists have to be able to offer credible clues to the resolution of discrepancies that they highlight. These of course lie in the gospel. Only when people know this will they trust the homilist sufficiently to engage themselves to any extent in the journey of the plot.

A good story maintains ambiguity for just long enough. So must homilies. A good homily will not rush to resolution, nor will it draw out the ambiguity. It will time the resolution so as to have the most impact on the listener. This timing is crucial. It is one of the variables learned only with experience. To be able to know when to invite a congregation to resolution is one of the necessary gifts for the effective exercise of the preaching ministry.

So while there is a place for preaching based upon a didactic form, it is my contention that *narrative form* provides us with the best model for achieving the aims of preaching outlined in the tradition.

It should be clear that I am not suggesting that homilies must always contain a story. What I am saying is that they will be most effective when they are constructed according to the structures and dynamics of story. Often an individual story is an effective and easy way to create the discrepancy at the beginning of a homily. But it is not the only way.

Because of the unconscious filters at work within our perceptive processes, to develop such a homiletical style will require discipline from the very beginning of our preparation. We need to keep in mind the components of narrative structure, for these will guide us as we listen to the sources of the homily's content.

Having examined the mechanics of narrative form, let us now turn to the text, the community and the preacher and see how the homily grows and develops.

Searching
the Sources

The Story of the Text

IT HAS BEEN said that there are only two certainties in life, death and taxes. To these the pastor in the parish can add next Sunday's homily! No sooner is one delivered than it is time to begin preparing the next. All of us have spent untold hours waiting for that creative insight to surface so that we can get down to the business of drafting a text. While no method or technique will remove the need for hard work in homily preparation, there are some tools available that may help us to channel our efforts.

Earlier I indicated that the sources for the content of the homily are threefold: the text, the community and the preacher. While we may enter this triangle through any one of these poles, most preachers I know usually begin by reading the text; and for that reason we will deal first with the story of the text.

This has both advantages and disadvantages. It allows the text "the inside running" in the creative process. By approaching the text first, there is every chance that the central insight of the homily will derive from it. As long as this is tested against the other two poles for authenticity and relevance there is no problem. If it is not tested, however, it can happen that the preacher falls into the trap of preaching "truths" that have little or no impact upon listeners. It is advisable then to vary where we begin our preparation each week.

Before making some suggestions as to how the text contributes to the homily let us step back briefly and look at how the text itself has developed, and what role it plays in the whole Christian endeavor.

The foundational event for the Christian faith is the historical life, death and resurrection of Jesus of Nazareth. Jesus saw his life as grounded in his *relationship* with his God which he described in the beautifully familiar term, Abba. This relationship filled him with a Spirit that allowed him to interpret humanness in an entirely unique way. He preached a Kingdom of God that was marked by forgiveness, compassion and unity. He was particularly concerned for the poor and the dispossessed and was able to offer them healing and freedom.

People were attracted to him both through his preaching and through the way he lived out his vision. When they met him they saw themselves differently and they saw their *relationship* with God differently. This new relationship empowered them to live a new life. They began to share in his Spirit. His followers celebrated their new fellowship with God and one another through sharing meals, which became a distinctive characteristic of the group. His preaching challenged many of the Jewish practices of his day which tended to fragment, isolate and eventually alienate certain groups of Jews. In the end, Jesus was put to death on a charge of blasphemy by the Jews and sedition by the Romans.

The death of Jesus profoundly changed the life of that fledgling group of Christians. Naturally they were shattered that the person who had brought so much freedom and peace into their lives was no longer with them. Then there was that magnificent experience of the first Easter morn when they became aware that Jesus lived. The Father he had spoken of had not deserted him in death and had indeed raised him to new life. From the way the first Christian communities spoke of the Ascension, it is clear they believed that Jesus, having been raised, had now returned to be with his Father.

As they continued to meet to remember, and to support one another, they became increasingly aware that while the historical Jesus was dead, and the risen Jesus had returned to the Father, the Spirit of Jesus continued to dwell in their midst. This Spirit stimulated and sustained the relationship begun in their experience with the historical Jesus. Individuals within the group, and the group as a whole, continued the preaching of the Kingdom begun by Jesus, and the power of the Spirit that shaped the life of Jesus continued to manifest itself through healing and liberating people. People were discovering the same relationship to God in and through the Spirit which those who had met the historical Jesus had discovered.

The presence of this Spirit always triggered memories of the historical Jesus and hence the Spirit was always seen in continuity with the historical Jesus. So much were the Spirit and Jesus intertwined that Paul virtually sees a functional identity between the Spirit and the risen Lord. For Paul, the risen Lord is seen mainly in terms of a new Spirit at work in people's lives. Initially, there was a strong expectation that Jesus would return to establish his Kingdom. But as time went on this expectation faded and the Christian community began to focus its attention more and more upon the presence of the Spirit in its midst.

A radical shift had occurred in the way Christians now encountered the Father. Those who met the historical Jesus found that in doing so they discovered within themselves a new Spirit which allowed them to enter into a new relationship with God as loving Father. Now that Jesus had died, people were discovering within themselves the Spirit of Jesus which reminded them of the historical Jesus who had revealed for them their intimate relationship with God the Father. People now lived in the Spirit and went *through* the Son to the Father. This is the way the first post-resurrection Christians met Jesus, and it is the way people meet him today. Most importantly for our considerations, it is the way the writers of the gospels met Jesus and through him discovered a new relationship with God.

The gospel writers were Christians of their day, living within active Christian communities. Along with their fellow Christians, they believed in the essential continuity between the historical Jesus and the Spirit at work in their lives and the lives of their communities. Consequently, they told the Christian story in such a way that the remembered elements of Jesus' earthly ministry would clarify the Spirit's urgings present in both the lives of individual community members and the community itself.

So on the one hand, we see Mark, writing for a persecuted community, presenting Jesus as the suffering Son of Man who will be exalted through his sufferings and return to judge the living and the dead. And on the other hand, Luke, writing for a community trying to live the Christian life in the society of the day, is more interested in presenting Jesus as the exemplar of the Christian life who prays, attends the Temple and forgives his executioners. The final judgment is not emphasized.

Different situations provoke different memories for each evangelist who then shapes the memory to speak to the specific situations. The evangelists were intent upon creating a relevant Jesus for their own communities, not a document that would be handed down through the ages. They simply told the story so that people would recognize the movement of the Spirit in their lives and so be led to the Father.

We could summarize by saying that the evangelists were perceptive members of early Christian communities with direct access through an oral tradition to the living memory of the historical Jesus. Within their own personal lives and within the life of their community, they experienced the creative movements of the Spirit. Like all religious experience, these no doubt primarily disclosed to the evangelists their intimate relationship with God, and had a depth that could be known only through the power of the imagination as I have previously described it, and adequately spoken about only in the languages of the imagination. The evangelists then tested these against the living memory of the historical Jesus in order to clarify and affirm the discerned presence of the Spirit. It was out of this process that the texts of the gospels developed.

While the evangelists were dealing with objective historical facts, their interest was biased by their faith and their own experience. They were more interested in helping people develop a relationship with God through Jesus than preserving a historical portrait. The story they tell is of how human life changes when it is lived out of a conscious relationship with Christ. This is a story of the heart, which can only be told in the language of metaphor. When they tell of Jesus healing a withered hand, they are speaking as much of the inner healing experienced through faith in the risen Lord, as they are of some historical event. Similarly all the images they attribute to Jesus, like "lamb", "shepherd" or "light", are metaphors that are trying to nuance their deep interpersonal relationship with the risen Lord in the Spirit.

Understanding this ferment that produced the text provides us with some clues as to how we might best approach the text in homily preparation. The most fundamental observation that needs to be made is to ask the question, "When we approach the text, who is speaking to whom?" Our culture, its language and the popular piety of our day, predisposes us to try to "figure out" the meaning of the text. Such an approach seems arrogant when the text at stake is the Word of God. Like the evangelists, we need to be modest in the face of God's Word. We make ourselves vulnerable to the text, and rather than our interpreting it, we allow it to interpret our lives and the life of our community. It is important that we approach the text as a *listener*.

To be able to listen appropriately requires us to appreciate the use by the evangelists of the language of the imagination. This is a gentle language that invites the listener to enter the story and feel it from the inside. Indeed, without willingness on the part of the listener, its truth often remains unheard. To hear what the evangelists are saying, it is necessary for us to be willing to enter the stories through our imaginations, and to respond to the insights that are disclosed to us.

Most significantly, the text is a document, spoken out of an experience of faith and heard only through the ears of faith. For too long, particularly in the Catholic tradition, the faithful surrendered their right to experience the text directly. They believed that the interpretation of the text belonged to the exegetes or the teaching authority of the Church. There developed a fear of the text that sent people searching for expert opinion before confidently submitting their lives to the text.

Because of this attitude, many treated the text as though it were a painting on the wall. They were inclined to *look at* it. The catechetical and homiletical style of earlier times tended to moralize the text, suggesting that each text had a particular meaning. Such a static understanding distilled from it much of its power and energy. Good homiletical practice will somehow invite people into the text in order to experience its power from within.

The fear of personally interacting with the text continues today. Many homilists are still inclined to first read expert commentaries before actually experiencing or exegeting the text themselves. Homilists need to accept the responsibility that the ministry involves. They are called to perpetuate the gospel message, not simply preserve it. They are to be gospel interpreters within the communities that have called them to this ministry.

This is not to deny the importance of biblical scholarship in the ministry of preaching. The better we are able to understand the context in which the gospels were written, the more accurately are we able to hear their message. Modern biblical scholarship has not only provided us with a fairly stark portrait of the historical Jesus, but it has also given us an appreciation of the many colors involved in the portrait of the Christ of faith in the gospels. Indeed, it is from biblical scholarship that my first suggestion for approaching the text comes.

Some Tools to Assist in Hearing the Story of the Text

Our most important guideline, when it comes to listening to the text, is to *give it time*. The following suggestions are aimed at improving the quality and effectiveness of our homilies. Indeed, rather than shorten the time of preparation they may well lengthen it! In view of the importance of the ministry of preaching, it is surprising to find out just how little time many spend in actually preparing a Sunday homily. To listen to and experience the meaning of the text takes time. It takes time to read the text closely, and it takes time to reflect upon it constructively. Homily preparation, needs to begin early in the week so that we are able to give the text time to wash over us.

A. Doing an Exegesis of the Text

The first task in approaching the text of the homily is to establish the meaning the text had in its original setting. While most colleges involved in the training of people for ministry today provide their students with some methods of exegesis, this was not always the case in the past, especially in the Catholic tradition. Consequently, there are many entrusted with the ministry of preaching who do not feel confident to prepare their own exegesis of a text. Exegesis establishes the original meaning of the text through a careful examination of the words, and the situation in which the text was actually written.

The following exegetical method is one that many have found manageable in a parish setting. I will use a variety of texts to exemplify this method. In the sample homily in Chapter Ten the method is used on the given text.

Each of the following steps will provide some insights into the meaning of the text. Some suggest it is best if a paraphrase of the passage is made after step 1. From subsequent steps, any changes that need to be made are noted. At the end of the process, a final paraphrase is made and it is this that is brought into dialogue with the life of the community and the preacher. This has merit, particularly when we are beginning with the method. After a little practice, it is usually sufficient simply to note what insights might come from each of the steps and at the conclusion write a working paraphrase.

1. READ THE TEXT CAREFULLY

Most texts need to be read a number of times in order to get their feel. The way the homilist first reacts to the text is most important. It is best if this initial reading is done in the translation that will be used in worship.

Particularly when beginning with the method, it is helpful to write a paraphrase of the text at this stage. Note the major themes and your own personal responses.

Next, note any textual variations in the footnotes. Originally the Scriptures were copied by hand and it was inevitable that variations would arise. Some of these variations are very significant, e.g., the oldest manuscripts conclude Mark's gospel at Ch. 16, vs. 8. The stories of the appearances of Christ in vs. 9–20 are a later addition. While often these may not affect the meaning of a passage, sometimes they can and so it is always worth checking. A rule of thumb in textual criticism is that the preferred reading is the one that best accounts for the others. Take Mk. 16,1. The Jerusalem Bible reads, "When the sabbath was over, . . ." and notes a variation, "When the sun had arisen . . .". In preferring the first, the translators obviously felt that the second phrase was probably included by a scribe either as a literary embellishment or because of a non-Jewish background.

Since most preachers do not have a facility with the original Greek, they have to depend upon English translations. It is important to remember that each translation is also an interpretation of the text.

Translations may be broadly grouped into two schools. The first group attempts to express the *thought* of the original in a fluent English form. An example would be the Jerusalem Bible. The second attempts to give a more literal translation of the original text, even though this may affect the English flow. The Revised Standard Version Bible would be in this group.

An example would be the Beatitudes in Mt. 5,1–12. The R.S.V. uses "blessed" and the J.B. uses "happy". In English this choice of word changes the "feel" of the text, which may be significant when we come to examine some other ways of appreciating it.

While often the textual variations and the variations in translations do not significantly affect the meaning of the text, they can sometimes provide valuable insights. Having read the translation to be used in worship, we need to consult a couple of other translations so as to gain a more rounded understanding of what the text is actually saying.

2. NOTE ANY SPECIFIC REFERENCES TO PEOPLE, PLACES, INSTITUTIONS AND CULTURAL OR RELIGIOUS PRACTICES

Most of us have heard these names and titles many times but often our understanding of them has remained vague. For example, to understand Mt. 17,9–13 it is essential to know the story of Elijah. It is helpful to know what characterized the various religious and social groups mentioned in the gospels: Pharisees, Scribes, Saducees, Herodians, Zealots, tax-collectors, centurions. It is helpful to know the various Jewish festivals, how they were celebrated and what they signified, e.g. Passover, Tabernacles. The geographical details are also important, e.g. the Decapolis and Samaria. These details and what they infer contribute substantially to the evangelist's message.

There are a number of excellent reference books that provide this information. One is the four volumes plus a supplement of *The Interpreters Dictionary of the Bible*. Another adequate but shorter work is John McKenzie's *Dictionary of the Bible*. Taking the few minutes needed to consult one of these works may well result in a significant insight into the meaning of the text.

3. NOTE THE WORDS OR PHRASES THAT STRIKE YOU AS EITHER SIGNIFICANT OR DIFFICULT TO UNDERSTAND

This step also requires careful reading. There is a richness and depth to the text that is deadened by repetition and familiarity. How often have we picked up a text and noticed a word or a phrase that we had never noticed previously? Or how often have we been in a Scripture discussion group when someone points out something that had completely escaped our attention? While sometimes this oversight occurs through lack of concentration, it may also indicate an aspect of our own lives that we are avoiding.

At this stage look particularly for qualifying words , phrases or sentences that affect the tone of the text. A good example would be the second miracle of the loaves in Mk. 8,1–10. Vs. 2 reads, "I feel sorry for all these people . . .". The word "sorry" or "compassion" in the R.S.V. is a significant word that needs to be understood.

4. WHAT ARE THE THEOLOGICALLY SIGNIFICANT TERMS, PHRASES AND THEMES IN THE PASSAGE?

Most passages will contain several technical terms or phrases which may require some research. In a passage like Mk. 8,34–9,1, which deals with the parousia, phrases like "Son of Man", "glory of His Father" and the whole of 9,1, "I tell you there are some standing here who will not face death before they see the Kingdom of God come with power" would require attention.

A good theological dictionary is essential for this. Within the gospels there is a great deal of variety in the way each evangelist uses specific terms. For example, there is a difference in the way each of the Synoptics understand the terms "Son of God" and "Kingdom of God". We need the assistance of specialist exegetes and biblical theologians to appreciate these differences so as to be able to take them into account in our own exegesis.

Once we have clarified these meanings, it helps to jot down the major themes in the passage. In Mk. 8, 34-9,1 some of these could be:

    a. Renunciation of self
    b. The cost of discipleship
    c. Loyalty to Christ and his message
    d. The position of Christ in the dispensation of salvation.

5. EXAMINE THE CONTEXT OF THE PASSAGE WITHIN THE GOSPEL AND COMPARE IT WITH PARALLELS IN OTHER GOSPELS

Because Scripture is only one component of worship, the passages read are often an extract from a larger gospel picture. Knowing the fuller context is important for it often nuances the meaning of the shorter text.

First there is the immediate context. An example would be the cure of the sick man at the pool of Bethzatha in John's gospel. The passage usually used in worship is from 5,1-15. However, it is vs. 16-47 which make it clear that the healing symbolizes the gift of life.

And then there is the wider context of the whole gospel. For example, on one level, John's gospel tells the story of how the pre-existent Word of God became incarnate in Jesus, and then returned to the glory of the Father through his passion, death, and resurrection. On a second symbolic level, it is a story about light encountering and overcoming darkness. It is only through these central symbols of the gospel that we are able to fully appreciate many of the stories and dialogues within it.

Because John's gospel essentially draws upon its own sources, there are not so many obvious parallels between it and the Synoptics. This is not the case with the Synoptics. Most scholars agree that Matthew and Luke had access to Mark and a common source termed Q. In addition, both had some original material of their own. Each of the evangelists wrote for a specific community and so shaped his material accordingly. The particular theological bias of each is probably best seen when we examine their gospels in parallel. The intention of each evangelist becomes clear when we see the way each evangelist selects or deletes common material. A work like Burton Throckmorton's *Gospel Parallels* is another essential tool for the homilist.

Take the Beatitudes in Mt. 5,3–12 and Lk. 6,20–23. Matthew, a Jew writing among and for Jews, has carefully crafted a gospel along rabbinic lines which is a dramatic account of the coming of the Kingdom in Jesus. To make his presentation of the Kingdom more complete in the Beatitudes, he includes other sayings of Jesus within this sermon. Luke, on the other hand, probably had a pagan background and wrote for a church in a Gentile setting. His is a compassionate gospel, particularly concerned for the outcast and the sinner. Consequently, he deletes matter that refers to Jewish laws and practices with which many of his readers would not be familiar. Hence the shortened version of the Beatitudes.

6. REFLECT UPON WHAT THE EVANGELIST IS TRYING TO SAY ABOUT JESUS IN THIS PASSAGE

To be able to answer the question, "What is the evangelist trying to say to his listeners about Jesus?", we need to clarify the historical circumstances of the particular gospel. This is an extension of what is done in the last step.

In answering this question it is good to keep in mind that there are a number of historical levels at which the passage has existed. Firstly, there was the actual historical experience in the life of Jesus that triggered this memory. We can ask, what was the significance of this event in the life of Jesus himself? Then there are the historical circumstances of the oral tradition that led to the inclusion of this particular memory. Finally, there are the historical circumstances that provoked the evangelist to use this particular matter in his gospel. While each of these levels may provide material for a homily, it is usually the last that is most helpful.

Take Mt. 10,26–33. Matthew was writing from within a church facing persecution by continuing to attend the synagogue. Through these words of Jesus, he was encouraging his listeners to openly confess Jesus, even though this would mean expulsion from the synagogue and social ostracism. They need not be afraid of their persecutors for the God of Jesus cares for them. It is this relationship that should be central in their lives and influence their attitudes and behavior.

7. Now Write Your Own Paraphrase of the Text

This is an important step. Writing is a discipline that helps us clarify vagueness in our thought. Even though we may have jotted down the various insights that each of the steps disclosed, it is necessary to pull them together by writing an actual paraphrase of the text. Without this, much of our hard work may be lost.

Once the exegesis is complete, compare it with the notes taken after your first reading of the text. Often we will be surprised at how a text discloses its fuller meaning through sustained reflection and study.

8. Compare Your Exegesis With a Good Commentary and Adjust Where Necessary

It is best to consult a commentary like *The Jerome Biblical Commentary* *after* we have done our own exegesis. We may be tempted to take a short cut and go straight to the commentary. However, a true appreciation of the text only comes after we have wrestled with it. The exegetical method provides a way of wrestling. If we consult a commentary before we do this, we will lose much of the "feel" for the text that comes from doing our own exegesis.

9. Examine the Other Readings and Look for Connections

Most worship ceremonies have more than one reading. The Church selects readings that are appropriate for the various seasons of its year. As well, the selection and sequence of the readings are designed so that over a period, worshiping Christians are exposed to the whole gospel. While I believe that the homily should normally be taken from the gospel other reading can often provide a backdrop. Consequently, once an exegesis of the gospel is completed, it is worth seeing firstly, how it may relate to the other readings, and secondly, how it relates to the particular season of the church's year.

B. Using the Exegesis

Once the exegesis is complete, we are in a position to hear the message of the text clearly. Remember that the text has little intrinsic value. Its value lies in the meaning it has when read by a person of faith. While accurately knowing what an evangelist may have said to his community is an essential first step, it is just that:

the first step. The all important next step is to be able to use these insights to critique the faith lives of people and communities today.

This is done through entering the text as though we were actually present at the time it was written. Let us use Mt. 10, 26–33 again.

Imagine yourself as a member of Matthew's community. This would mean you were of Jewish origin and a recent convert to the Christian faith. There is every chance that the initial excitement had waned and now you are faced with living the Christian life in a hostile Jewish environment. Contributing to the tension is the weekly attendance at the synagogue, which has been part and parcel of your life. Now you are confronted with the choice of either denying Christ and the freedom that Christian faith has brought, or acknowledging him and being expelled from the synagogue as a heretic and having to live as one of a despised minority within the Jewish community. It is a situation potentially charged with many strong feelings: fear, anxiety, self-pity, hope, camaraderie. Allow yourself to feel these emotions in your imagination.

Having created this atmosphere, read the text and listen for insights. One that struck me comes from vs. 28. We need to fear that person who can destroy not only our body but also our soul or inner self. Our exegesis would have disclosed to us that this is a reference to ourselves. All of a sudden we are aware of a new sense of freedom that makes us feel our destiny is in our own hands. If we choose to remain faithful to our Christian values and attitudes in our everyday living, we will know the care of our Father and the freedom that brings, even though we may be persecuted. Imagine the relief such an insight would effect, given the circumstances of the original listeners.

Now take this felt insight and abstract from it the general principles involved. One would be that so often in difficult, and indeed not so difficult situations, we surrender our freedom of choice to our external circumstances. In so doing, we lose our true identity, which is the goal of our Christian faith, and become a prisoner to the situation.

Now search your own personal lived experience and the experience of your community to test the truth of this insight. (How to go about this is addressed in subsequent chapters.) Maybe you remember a time when this happened to you. Recreate the experience in your imagination, allowing the feelings to surface. Now listen to what the insight may have to say to you in those circumstances. From within our Australian community experience, the principle offers some sound guidance. As a nation, we are currently spending more than we earn. Collectively we may be surrendering our freedom in order to satisfy our immediate desires.

We will usually find that this process generates the seeds of a good homily.

C. Approaching the Text as Story

Once we have completed our exegesis, we are able to interact with the text much more freely. The first method we suggested for using the text focuses its attention upon the meaning the evangelist intended for his listeners. The following methods use the text to imaginatively reconstruct the historical scene in the time of Jesus.

Both methods use the same imaginative process. They differ only in *where* attention is focused.

With the knowledge gleaned from the exegesis, imagine yourself as one of the characters. Often this will simply require you to imagine you are as one of the crowd that listened to Jesus. Sometimes it will mean imagining yourself as a particular individual or one of the disciples. Feel with the characters as the story unfolds. Listen carefully to how he or she interacts with Jesus and others: what each says to the other; how each feels; how each responds to the interaction. Note these feelings and any insights that strike you. It is important to enter the stories through the Jesus figure as well as the other characters. This helps us to feel what it is like to live and think as Jesus did.

As in the last method, after experiencing the text, try to abstract the principles it might contain.

Now search your own experience and the experience of the community for situations which may be very different in circumstance but which have a "feel" to them that is similar to that of the recreated gospel setting. Hold these experiences in tension with the principles discerned from the gospel text and listen for insights.

The first method focuses upon the cultural and social setting of the text. Take Lk. 10,25-37. Jesus is confronted by a Jewish lawyer and in response to the question, "Who is my neighbor?" tells the story of the Good Samaritan. In the story Jesus brings together what were, for the Jews listening to him, two incompatible concepts: "good" and "Samaritan". Jews of that day took for granted that Samaritans were inferior to them. This cultural setting adds to the poignancy of the story for the listeners.

One principle the passage highlights is how destructive prejudice can be in our lives. So often it can prevent us from seeing where God is truly at work. It is only in becoming conscious of our prejudice that we can become free of its power over us.

The white Australian attitude to Aboriginal people has a "feel" similar to the gospel setting. Generally it is presumed that the white Western way of doing things is best. Rarely, if ever, has it been suggested that white Australians may learn from Aboriginals.

The passage challenges this prejudice. Maybe God dwells more in Aboriginal ways than white ways. At least we need to examine our attitudes in this regard.

The second method, while using the same steps for entering the text, concentrates upon the interactions of the characters within the story itself. Our appreciation of these interactions is deepened by the information provided by the exegesis.

In the story of the cure of the centurion's servant (Lk. 7,1–10), we have Jesus interacting initially with the Jewish elders and then with the messengers from the centurion. In this second interaction we read that Jesus was "astonished" at the faith of the centurion.

This highlights the principle that ours is a God of surprises, to be found in the most unexpected of places.

Most of us would not have to look far in our lives to know the truth of this. A more relevant question may well be, "How long is it since I have been surprised by God?". Maybe there is a need within us to dispose ourselves better to receive the surprises of God.

One of the great bonuses of being entrusted with the ministry of preaching is that it keeps us in close personal contact with the Scriptures. The time spent in wrestling with the text often provides a lot more than just a good homily. Many preachers would testify that homily preparation has often been a time of encounter with God. Each of the methods above are as helpful for personal prayer as they are for homily preparation.

While exegeting the text may take most of the preparation time, we must remember it is but one of the sources. Just as important are the community's experience and the experience of the preacher. It is through the interaction of all three poles that good homilies are born. Let us now turn our attention to the community.

CHAPTER SEVEN

The Story of the Community

THERE IS A memorable scene in that delightfully human play *Mass Appeal* in which the pastor and the assistant pastor are discussing the needs of their community. The assistant turns to the pastor and says something like, "I love these people and I know what they can become!". And the old pastor replies, "Ah yes! But what about what they are now?"

It is into the actual world of individual people and specific communities that the preacher is called to bring the light of the Word of God. Entry into this world cannot be presumed by the preacher. While the Sunday congregation is a captive audience physically, they will allow the preacher into their inner worlds only if they know that he or she will speak about issues that are presently important for them. Being able to discern, understand, feel and articulate these needs is essential for effective preaching.

The relationship between a preacher and his or her people is something very special. While the institutional and liturgical structure provide the setting for the relationship, its inner core is shaped by the personal interaction between a preacher and his or her audience.

How homilists view themselves in relationship to their communities will influence both the matter of a homily and the manner in which it is communicated. The expectations of people play a significant role in this regard. It can sometimes happen that preachers become isolated from their communities through excessive respect. Within the Catholic tradition, and I suspect the same may be true within other traditions, there has been a tendency for parishioners to look upon their ministers as "holy people", with special insight into the Christian message and a special wisdom about how the Christian life should be lived.

It is easy for a minister to unconsciously accept this projection. As a result, at least unconsciously, a framework of relationship is established that sees the minister as being "apart" from the community and charged with the responsibility of bringing it some of the insight and wisdom he or she has acquired separate from the community. The pastor is like the potter, and the people are like the clay. In the Catholic tradition, this mindset is supported symbolically when pastors are appointed without the consent and approval of the local community.

This style of relationship predisposes a preacher to "look at" the experience of a community. It is easy for them to become prey to their own personal "filters" in discerning and assessing this experience. Ideals can begin to play an inordinate role in the way a preacher handles the matter of the homily. This attitude may also affect the manner of delivery. Some preachers have a "preaching voice" very different to their conversational voice. The formality of their language and their style of expression is tinged with more than a touch of "holy unreality".

Today there seems to be a healthy shift occurring in the expectations people have of their ministers and in the view ministers have of themselves. More and more people view their ministers as "fellow-travellers" on this journey of life. They certainly see that the special gifts these ministers have, and the training they have received, make them important to the community. Their importance, however, lies not in their bringing something from outside the community, but from living within it and reflecting upon that experience, thereby uncovering the already present Spirit.

These expectations contribute to a different style of relationship between preachers and their people. Because there is not the same idealism as in the previous set of expectations, there is room for a much more personal interaction. The preacher is able to manifest his or her own personal struggles within the community and seek its support. This will often lead to a relationship in which community members feel free to talk with their ministers about the "unholy" worries and concerns in life that may well contribute to the matter dealt with in homilies. Such a relationship can also affect the style of delivery. It will tend to be more conversational; a sharing between friends on the same journey. The homily becomes like the light of dawn: it brings the light that allows us to see what was there all along but hidden because of darkness.

The reality for most preachers today would be that their relationship with their community lies somewhere in between these two styles. Reflecting upon the styles may clarify for us where we actually are, and then free us to decide whether it is where we want to be and what influence it is having upon our preaching.

Getting to know our communities well enough to be able to assist them to understand their lives in the light of the gospel is becoming increasingly difficult. Christian communities function within a culture and take on many of the characteristics of that culture. Ours is a world short of time. As more and more demands are being placed upon people, there is an increasing need to use time efficiently. The way local churches function in their day-to-day life has not escaped these cultural influences.

Many pastors these days have taken on something of an executive role. A good deal of their time is spent in their office. Parishioners tend to make appointments and come to the parish office to see them. Ministries within the community are usually organized through meetings that take up much of the pastor's time.

These developments have affected the way pastors get to know the people of their communities. Anyone who has worked for any length of time in a local church will know that most people have a "church mask". They wear this when interacting in the various church settings: worship, meetings, speaking with the pastor or other parishioners, and the like. The interests and concerns they express in these circumstances invariably and understandably will not include all of the interests and concerns they have when in their own homes.

Getting to know parishioners "on their own turf" would seem to be essential if preachers are to deal with the real interests and concerns of their communities. Time has to be available for preachers to visit with people in their own homes so that they can hear their real needs. Where the preacher is also the pastor, this may well mean a change in the parish organization and administration.

As long as they are alert to the "church mask", preachers can also learn much from day-to-day interactions with parishioners. By carefully listening to what is said and how it is said, the preacher can discern the needs of people.

There is much to recommend a preacher using a group to assist in the preparation of the Sunday homily. The ministry belongs to the community rather than the individual preacher, and so it is reasonable for him or her to seek and obtain some assistance from the community. It may be a group specially established for this purpose.

I have always favored the use of already functioning prayer groups or Scripture discussion groups in the parish. A preacher can receive tremendous assistance in homily preparation if he or she is able to listen to the members of these groups reflecting on their lives in the light of the following Sunday's gospel.

The preacher is able to approach the experience of individuals and the community in many different ways, but most could be collated under two general headings: direct and indirect. Both these approaches are used by the Jesus of the gospels in his preaching. Circumstances would determine which approach is more appropriate.

Often Jesus is found directly addressing a particular behavior or attitude. In Lk. 7,36–50, he praises the love of the woman who had washed and anointed his feet, using the situation to answer the criticisms of Simon and to teach about the role of forgiveness in love. In the curing of the centurion's servant in Lk. 7,1–10, Jesus openly states his admiration for the centurion's faith.

Preachers too may sometimes choose to address directly both the positive and negative experience of their people. When this approach is used, it is important for the preacher to exercise prudence in the selection of experiences and to be extremely sensitive to confidentiality. Confidences can be broken by inference as much as direct reference and prudence would suggest that the preacher checks matter which may be sensitive with a trusted friend or mentor.

The second way of approaching the community's experience is well summed up in Kierkegaard's theory of indirect communication:

One day Kierkegaard was attending a funeral and after the interment he accidently overheard a grandfather talking to his grandson about death and resurrection. Kierkegaard was deeply moved. As he reflected upon this experience, he began to realize that in the "overhearing" he was provided with enough distance for him to participate in the story himself. It gave him space to reflect upon his own death.

We could point to a number of pastoral situations when this "overhearing" happens. There is probably none more obvious than when adults attend children's liturgies. How often have you heard adults say how the liturgy touched them! One of the reasons would be that because they were attending a liturgy for children, they were given enough space to be able to overhear their own story in what was said. Even with the variety of opinion surrounding Jesus' use of parables, most would see that they provided a way for people to "overhear" their own stories in terms of the Kingdom.

A preacher can very effectively use this indirect approach in dealing with the experience of people. Sometimes it is better to approach an experience or attitude by telling another story that allows people to "overhear" their own experience. It is particularly effective when the preacher perceives that a destructive attitude or behavior is so painful that a person, or a community, is unable to address it and may actually deny it.

Like all ministry, preaching focuses upon both the presence and the absence of the Kingdom. Human living is this complex mix of both sin and grace. Twenty years ago it would be fair to say that sin was usually the point of departure for most homilies. A good deal of the preaching of my childhood and adolescence was devoted to making people aware of the "sin" of their lives in the hope of enticing them to change. Guilt and remorse were used to provide motivation. Again speaking from my own Catholic tradition, there has been a change of emphasis. Today homilies tend to stress the love and compassion of God.

This shift has sound psychological and theological foundations. All Christian living grows out of an awareness of the presence of God in our lives. Grounded in this presence, we are better able to confront our sinfulness and allow the attitudes and values of the gospel to influence our lives more comprehensively.

Despite this new emphasis, sin will always remain, and indeed *needs* to remain, a central theme for preachers. The ministry of preaching is not about making people "feel" better for having come to Sunday worship. It is about the real, lived experiences of life and how the Christian gospel can help us interpret these. Whether people are prepared to admit it or not, some of these are destructive and sinful. So even though people may not wish their preachers to articulate these selfish and hurtful behaviors, doing so will always remain integral to the ministry.

St Vincent de Paul once said, "It is only when the poor feel your love that they will forgive you for your gift of bread and soup." Of course every time we give something to them we remind them that they are poor and dependent. For the homilist, the saying could well be rephrased: "It is only when they feel your love that people will forgive you for reminding them that they are selfish and hurtful to one another." People will usually allow a homilist into these sensitive areas of their lives only after they know that he or she loves them, and can be trusted to remain with them in their struggles.

The relationship between preachers and people is forged on many fronts. We should never underestimate the influence the homily itself has in the establishment of relationships. For many, it is the experience upon which they will judge whether a pastor is compassionate and approachable or judgmental and distant. Most preachers are also pastors and so what they say in homilies, and how they say it, is heard against the background of how they care for people in other ministries. It is from this broader experience that most will decide whether a preacher really loves them and whether they can trust him or her with those most fragile areas of their lives.

I was fortunate to learn the truth of this very early in my presbyteral ministry. In my first appointment I was sent to a parish in which there had only been one pastor. The parish was in a developing part of Toowoomba and had been cut off from the Cathedral ten years previously. The parish, people, and pastor had all grown together. This man may have known little of the theory of community building, but he knew a great deal about how a pastor should love his people. He had laughed with them and cried with them, fought with them and been forgiven by them, suffered their criticisms and forgiven them. Together they had worked to make that part of the world a better place to live. Theirs was a relationship marked by warm affection and deep respect.

Naturally, all of his ministry was influenced by his love for the community. In terms of preaching it meant that he loved his people too much to not prepare his homilies thoroughly. He had been ordained thirty years at that time, and still he wrote his homilies word for word. When he spoke, people listened. They knew he had something worthwhile to say. His love for his people meant also, that he was able to deal with both their positive and negative experiences.

I heard him preach on destructive behavior in the community

and I heard people afterwards speak of a need to change! I learned that when people know their preacher loves them, they will allow him or her into those most vulnerable areas of their lives.

While individual preachers may show us how to deal with the negative aspects of our lives, each is probably only giving a personal appropriation of the paradigm contained in John's story of the woman at the well. Here Jesus directly addressed the destructive behavior of the woman. But he did it in a way that did not cripple her with guilt or remorse. Indeed, his approach encouraged her to ask how she might live differently.

As with the ministry of Jesus, there is no place for encouraging the crippling emotions of guilt and remorse in the ministry of preaching. People's sinfulness needs to be addressed, but only in order that they may be invited to know a new freedom and a new peace. Like the woman at the well, people may go out and say, "Come and meet a man who told me all things about myself!"

Attending to the Experience of the Community and its People

A few questions asked at the beginning of preparation can help to ensure the relevance of the homily for the listeners. Try to answer the questions from the perspective of the congregation. If you are not sure, it may be worth asking around.

THE WORLD AND THE NATION

What is happening in the world, the nation and the state at present?

What are the headlines in the newspaper?

Which news reports are people talking about?

Are there some events being ignored? Why?

On which of these issues is there consensus in the community?

On which of these issues is there controversy?

What is fueling the controversy?

What is the general mood of the community at present with respect to these issues?

The Congregation

Who will be present at this worship?

What will be the age group, family situations, ethnic make-up etc.?

What sort of a theological and faith "feel" will the community have?

What is the present liturgical time and what does this mean to the people?

Has anything significant happened in the community recently? How have people responded?

What are the present preoccupations within the community: occasions to celebrate, problems, significant ministerial activities, etc.?

The Preacher

How do I feel about the community at present?

Do I share the community's interests and concerns?

These are just a few of the questions we may ask. They will give us an idea of what people have been talking and thinking about for the last week or so. To know this is an essential first step in homily preparation. The homilist's interest in the experience of people, however, goes well beyond being able to simply describe their external behavior and expressed opinions. Behind these there is a whole structure of meaning that shapes particular opinions and behavior. It is this world that is of most interest to the preacher.

Uncovering the Assumptive World of People

The Christian message is essentially to do with the *meaning* of life. All ministry, and particularly the ministry of preaching, is the means by which this message is communicated. The Christian message aims at promoting a particular way of being human. It does this by recognizing, uncovering, and affirming the presence of the Kingdom of God in people's lives. The Kingdom exists where the personal and social behavior of people bears what may be termed the "mark of God". Having experienced its freedom in their own lives, Christians are motivated and charged with the responsibility of creating a society whose structures nurture the growth of this Kingdom within individuals.

Like all human behavior, Kingdom behavior is grounded in a set of assumptions about the nature and goal of human life. Fundamental to these is the way Christians understand their relationship with God. These Kingdom assumptions, attitudes and values underpinned the life of the historical Jesus, and are preserved in the faith stories of the gospel. From these stories Christians are able to test the authenticity of their own assumptive worlds.

All human actions, and particularly significant human actions, are like an iceberg: there are many levels below the surface which cannot be seen that shape what happens above the surface. Every act posits a set of assumptions and presuppositions that conditions the way people respond to and make meaning of the experiences of their lives. People are aware of some of these assumptions for they have freely and consciously chosen to live out of them. Others lie deep in the unconscious, available to the conscious only through the language of symbols and metaphors. Depth psychologists like Freud and Jung have alerted us to the power of these unconscious assumptions. As we have said, it is to this assumptive world in both its conscious and unconscious dimension that the Christian message addresses itself. In attending to this world, preachers are called to listen with special ears.

It would be impossible and inappropriate to try and describe all the influences that might contribute to the way people make meaning of their experiences. Many of them provide the focus of attention of the various disciplines of the social sciences. A sound knowledge of these is invaluable for the homilist. However, a brief description of some of the dimensions of human life, shared by all, that contribute to the meaning-making process, is needed in order to understand how we are to listen to people as they tell of their experience.

To begin with, there is the inner world of a person. This contributes more than anything else to the way a person responds to the circumstances of life. From this inner world people derive their identity and sense of self-worth. It is a created world that develops from birth as a person absorbs and interrelates with the personal, social, cultural and natural world in which he or she lives. It is a world that is constantly changing throughout life.

Most of the interactions that are important to people happen in their relationships with those significant in their lives. As the result of these, they tend to adopt stances towards life and other people. If someone experiences these interactions positively, there is every chance he or she will view other people generally in a positive light. Intimacy with others will not be a threat. If, on the other hand, these interactions with significant others are negative, people become disposed to be wary of others and will often struggle to trust them in the more vulnerable areas of their lives.

Then there are the social settings in which people live out their lives: the workplace, the church they belong to, the social club, the sports club and the like. Each of these groups has a set of operating assumptions, attitudes and values. The personal assumptions, attitudes and values of an individual dialogue with these, and the result is usually a modification on the part of both the group and the individual.

There is also the society and culture in which people live. The influence of culture over their attitudes and values is much more extensive than most would appreciate. Culture provides what is termed a "collective consciousness". Much of the experience of people is understood according to a set of attitudes and values, taken for granted and never questioned, that are absorbed from the society in which people live. They are simply "the way things are done around here". People only become conscious of them when an experience, such as travel, or another person, such as a homilist, draws their attention to them.

Finally, we are influenced by the physical environment in which we live. All would be aware of the differences between life in a city and life in the country. Different aspects of life interest us depending on where we live. People use the images and symbols that surround them to understand their experience and to express them. Since the physical environment provides so many of these, it stands to reason that it will influence the meaning world of people.

All of these dimensions of life contribute to the assumptions, attitudes and values from which people make meaning of their experience. All, or any one, may disclose an important key that will uncover fundamental assumptions with which the Christian message can dialogue. In listening to their people, homilists need to remain ever alert to this complex mix that forms the basis of people's assumptions, attitudes and values.

People experience God in and through each of these environments. They provide the "stuff" of religious experience and the images and symbols used to express that experience. This is a real challenge to the Christian minister. Often the language people use to speak of their experience of God or their relationship with God is not "religious". A good minister has the skill to be able to recognize when this happens. A telltale clue is when people use the words, "Life is like . . .".

There has never been a more public example of this than when the former prime minister, Malcolm Fraser, made his famous statement, "Life wasn't meant to be easy!" It was spoken as a throwaway phrase, but said much about how Fraser interpreted human experience. The fact that it became enshrined in Australian folklore means that it struck a cord with people who unconsciously shared this understanding of life. Once we learn to "hear" the assumptions involved in these sorts of statements, then we are able to respond to them with Christian perception.

Some Tools for Uncovering this Assumptive World

A. Social Analysis

There are a number of ways of analyzing people's experience that can assist a homilist in uncovering the assumptive world of people. A good way to begin is to do some sort of social analysis of the community. This is not such a difficult task, but it does require accurate information. Many have been amazed by what they have found through a simple analysis. What they *thought* was the case and what they found to be the case were very different.

FIRST ATTEND TO THE CULTURAL ATMOSPHERE OF THE COMMUNITY

What races make up the congregation?

What are the cultural characteristics of each of these races?

How closely knit are each of the groups?

Where are the harmonious interactions between the groups?

Where are the obvious cultural "clashes"?

What are the fundamental questions underlying these clashes?

These types of questions are becoming more and more important in city parishes in Australia as the character of the population becomes more and more multicultural.

NEXT LOOK AT THE SOCIAL ATMOSPHERE OF THE COMMUNITY

What is the breakdown of the group in terms of age?

What is the breakdown in terms of family structures (two parents with 1, 2, 3 children, etc., single parents with 1, 2, 3 children, etc.)?

What is the breakdown in terms of income (lower, middle, upper)?

What is the breakdown in housing (own home, renting a house, renting an apartment, public housing)?

What are the education levels of people (university educated, have a trade, high school, less than high school)?

What type of work are the majority engaged in (management, white collar, public service, blue collar trades, blue collar workers, domestic duties)?

What are the major social needs in the area (financial, unemployment, race, youth, aged, single parents, drugs, alcohol, vandalism, etc.)?

As a group, what are the dominant values that motivate (individualism, rationalism, conformism, materialism, status, consumerism, etc.)?

What is the "atmosphere" of the group (contented, uneasy)?

EXAMINE THE ENVIRONMENT

What is the nature of the physical environment (inner city, suburban, town-country, country)?

What public spaces are there and how are they used?

Who uses them?

How would you summarize the natural environment (beautiful, crowded, dirty, etc.)?

NOW LOOK AT THE LEADERSHIP IN THE COMMUNITY

How involved are people in political parties?

Who are the elected representatives?

How do they perform in the community?

Who are the influential people in the community?

What is their background?

Why are they influential?

What influence do local organizations have in the community?

What sway does the media have over the formulation of community values?

What biases are expressed in the local media?

FINALLY LOOK TO THE ROLE OF THE LOCAL CHURCHES WITHIN THE COMMUNITY

What is the breakdown, in terms of numbers and personnel, of the various traditions?

How do the various churches dispose of their resources: are they used for "internal" church matters or are they used for the good of the wider community?

Do these work together or at odds with each other?

How are the churches regarded by the wider community?

What is the strength of church leadership?

What is the morale of full-time workers?

This data becomes invaluable for reflecting upon how people interpret their experience. It also allows the homilist to understand better the actual constitution of his or her congregation and some of the influences that affect their day-to-day living. How often have we heard a preacher give a homily on the family as the basic unit of society when his or her congregation consists largely of single people and single-parent families? A homilist who has done a social analysis is in a much better position to be aware of the real interests and concerns of his listeners.

B. Understanding the Language and Symbols of the Community

Modern communication theory has alerted us to the complexity of the communication act. All of us have known the experience in preaching when we have said one thing and people have heard something entirely different. At times this may be the Spirit at work. More often it is because we are working out of a different world of meaning to those who listen to us. What we mean when we use a word is not what it means when they hear it.

A very helpful tool for understanding the communication act is the Information Theory Triangle. I first discovered this in Raymond Collins's book, *Models of Theological Reflection*. The triangle was developed by the science of semiotics which studies how signs signify and communicate their meaning. Of course, the fundamental symbol system in which we all participate is language and so it is an appropriate tool to use in assessing verbal communication. I have also found it helpful in examining the actions and gestures of individuals. Often it can alert us to a discrepancy between behavior and rhetoric in a particular situation.

The following diagram sets out the triangle:

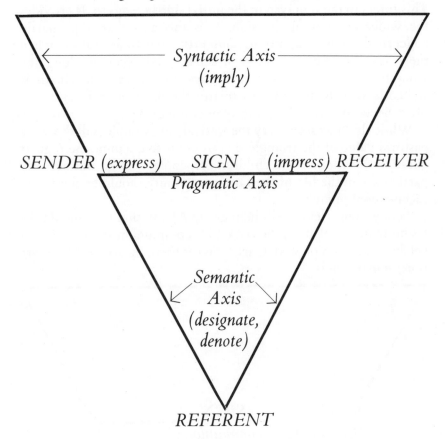

Communication occurs when a *sender* expresses a *sign* that impresses the *receiver*. The line between these two is referred to as the *pragmatic* axis. The verbs that best describe what happens along this axis are "express" for the sender and "impress" for the receiver. Along this axis there needs to be some form of physical contact, either directly or indirectly, such as a letter or telephone.

At the point of the triangle below this line is the *referent*. The relationship between the *sign* and the *referent* is known as the *semantic* axis. Semantics studies the relationship between a sign and what it signifies. Obviously, if there is to be effective communication, there needs to be agreement between the sender and the receiver along this semantic axis. Otherwise what is signified for the sender is different from what is signified for the receiver.

Above the pragmatic axis is what is termed the *syntactic* axis. This refers to the sign system the initial sign belongs to. It provides the wider context of the sign. It is this axis that is primarily concerned with assumptions and presuppositions. Often when there is a discrepancy between sender and receiver along the semantic axis, it can be traced back to a divergence in their syntactic worlds. In order to rectify the differing referents it is often necessary to address the syntactic worlds.

While this may seem very theoretical, an example will show the pastoral value of the triangle. Let us use it to examine the regular question of whether the children of people who do not actively participate in the life of the faith community should be invited to receive communion.

Today, some (let us call them group A), say that they should not be invited. In terms of the triangle, communion is the *sign* that celebrates our union with Christ. So for them the *referent* of the *sign* is *union with Christ*.

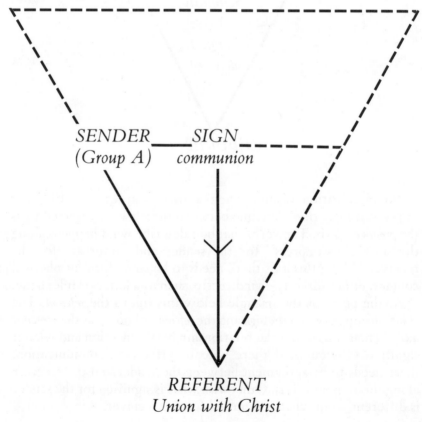

SENDER___SIGN___
(Group A)   communion

REFERENT
Union with Christ

The *union with Christ* celebrated in communion not only implies an active role in the life of the faith community, but can be properly understood only in terms of it. This constitutes the *syntactic* world of Group A.

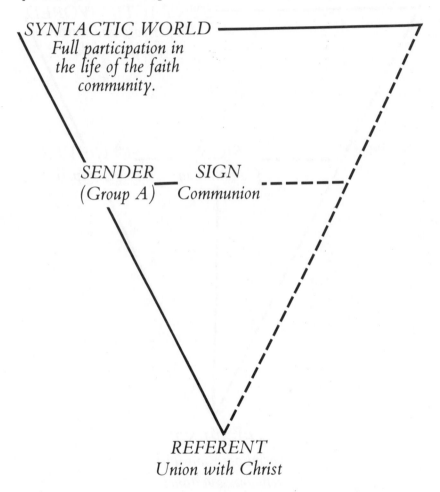

SYNTACTIC WORLD
Full participation in
the life of the faith
community.

SENDER   *SIGN*
(Group A) *Communion*

REFERENT
Union with Christ

But there is another group (Group B) who see things differently. Communion for them is more a social occasion in a religious setting. While there may be a vague understanding of its importance in a person's relationship with Christ, this is not the primary focus. Further, since these people would not want to do anything that might alienate their children from their peers, if most in the class are going to receive communion they too would want their children to participate. Encouraging their child to receive communion

91

communion is seen as part and parcel of the nurture and care good parents provide.

The triangle looks very different for this group.

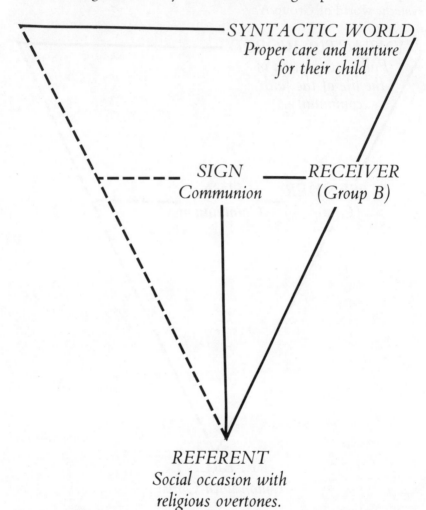

SYNTACTIC WORLD
Proper care and nurture
for their child

SIGN ———*RECEIVER*
Communion *(Group B)*

REFERENT
Social occasion with
religious overtones.

To clarify the example, let's say that Group A represents a pastoral team. Someone from Group B asks for communion for their child. Group A, using their *syntactic world*, considers it inappropriate and says, "no". The person from Group B hears the reply from their *syntactic world* (care and nurture, etc.) and goes away saying the pastoral team does not care for their child!

Of course this is not what was intended by the pastoral team.

However, because of the difference between the *syntactic worlds* of the two, and the consequent difference in the *referents* to the *sign*, "communion", there is a breakdown in communication, often with tragic consequences for both parties.

While learning to use the triangle may take some practice, I believe it is well worth the effort. Uncovering the *syntactic world* of people tells us a great deal about the basis of their assumptions and attitudes, which are of specific interest to the ministry of preaching.

There would be value in using the triangle to reflect upon the following questions:

How is the word "God" referred to? Is the syntactic world of its usage that of "judge" or "lover"?

What makes a person "good"? External success or personal integrity?

What is the purpose of the family? Is it child focused or adult focused?

Which are the most important age groups in the community? Children, youth, mid-life, aged?

What is the community's attitude to outsiders? Judging or loving?

C. Listening to a Particular Pastoral Experience

While it is important to attend to the social and community atmosphere in which people live, the best way for preachers to inhabit the world of their people is by carefully listening to individuals as they tell of their experiences. The following method for reflecting upon an individual ministerial experience may help.

First recreate the experience through your memory and imagination. While a full verbatim form may not always be necessary, when first using this method it is highly recommended. This involves recording the conversation word for word and noting your own feelings as well as the non-verbal gestures of the other person. This exercise is also helpful in honing our empathetic listening skills which tend to diminish in the rush and bustle of parish ministry.

ATTEND TO THE SOCIAL BACKGROUND OF THE PERSON

What are the significant social relationships in their lives?

How much value do they place upon these relationships?

What gives these relationships value?

What is their educational background?

What is their financial situation?

What constitutes success in life for them?

What is their employment situation (management, employee, trade, white collar, blue collar)?

What value do they place on their work?

How much satisfaction do they get from work?

LISTEN FOR THEIR MORAL STANCE

What constitutes "good" and "bad" for them?

Are they motivated from within or without?

What energizes them in their behavior?

How do they regard others and how does this compare with the way they regard the significant people in their lives?

What is their attitude to authority?

Are they dependent or self-motivated?

LISTEN FOR THE ROLE OF THE TRANSCENDENT IN THEIR LIVES

What appears to be the essential purpose in life for them?

How does their present experience fit with this purpose in life?

How do they view the relationship between God and creation?

Is God imminent or transcendent or both?

How do they view the relationship between God and people?

Do they see the world as good or bad?

How do they see their own relationship with God?

Do they see their humanness as good or bad?

Is the way they talk about God consistent with the way they act in life?

How do they communicate with God?

How and where does their God communicate with them?

What is the primary source of their belief system?

What is their relationship with organized religion?

Where does the balance of authority lie here (within or without)?

How effectively are they able to use their belief system to interpret this present experience?

FINALLY, TRY TO FIND AN APPROPRIATE IMAGE THAT SUMS UP THE EXPERIENCE AND ITS MEANING

Listen to the experience through the image to see if it sheds any insight upon the experience.

Naturally the answers to most of these questions will be found only through inference. It is necessary therefore to hasten slowly in drawing definite conclusions. Insights may need to be checked against similar experiences of other people. However, serious reflection upon a person's experience through these questions will disclose a good deal about the assumptive world of that person. It will probably also disclose a good deal about our own assumptive world as well. Both are invaluable to the preacher.

Using the Insights

Once homilists are able to establish something of the assumptive world of their listeners they are well placed to bring this to the gaze of the gospel. This can be done by following these simple steps which are just a reversal in order of the method suggested in the use of the Scriptural text.

From a reflection upon the experiences of people, describe the underlying assumptions, attitudes, and values that inform and shape their individual behavior.

Allow any Scripture texts that seem to resonate with these principles to surface from your memory.

Discern the underlying principles in these texts through the methods suggested.

Allow the text and its principles to dialogue with the experience and its principles and *listen* for insights.

All of this may seem a little daunting. Something such as social analysis would only be done periodically. Examining language and symbols would be helpful if there was a shift in language use or behavioral practice. However it is done, it is absolutely essential that homilists inhabit the world of their listeners. Only then will people entrust them with those deepest areas of their lives where meaning is born.

The Story of the Preacher

I WELL REMEMBER an evening a couple of years ago when I was sitting with a group of priests and students in the common room at St Paul's Seminary. The conversation had ranged over a number of subjects and for a time centered around the ministry of preaching. In just three comments volumes were spoken about how preachers view their ministry. The comments ran something like this:

"I find it a real drag. Week after week having to get up and say something! It's a real strain. But I got onto a homily service and a few books of homilies and with them I manage."

"No, it's not like that for me. I really enjoy it. I probably get more satisfaction from preaching than from most other ministries I am involved in. Mind you, I have to work at it but still it's good."

"For the first couple of years I thought I was telling them about the gospel. But I realise now I was really telling them my own story. Not that I talked very often about my own experience. I guess that's just part of the deal."

I am convinced of the truth of the last comment. The faith of preachers and their attitude to the ministry will largely determine what and how they preach. Our own stories will have at least as much influence upon our homilies as both the text and the concerns of the community. And our own stories of faith will be told either directly or indirectly as long as we stand up in front of our people Sunday after Sunday.

Preachers are made vulnerable by their ministry. When they preach, they risk disclosing their own relationship with God and how they understand life. While that risk should never be taken lightly it will, nonetheless, always need to be taken as long as the Word of God needs to be proclaimed.

Being able to articulate the specific characteristics of their faith is important for preachers. The following questions may help.

> Where, when, and with whom do I experience God most regularly?
>
> When was my last experience of God?
>
> What are the significant spiritual experiences of my life?
>
> What difference does my faith make to my day-to-day living?
>
> What was the last decision I made that was directly influenced by my faith?
>
> Who is Jesus for me?
>
> How, when, and where do I contact him?
>
> What kind of relationship do I have with him?
>
> How important is the community to my faith?
>
> What style of relationship do I have with the community?
>
> What characters in the Scriptures do I identify with? Why?
>
> What is it about my faith that I really want to share with others?
>
> Am I able to talk about my faith without embarrassment?
>
> Do I encourage others to talk about their faith?
>
> Do I respect others' beliefs when they differ from my own?

Through these types of questions preachers are able to define for themselves the contours of their own faith. Clarity in their own minds about its value and how it actually operates will sharpen preachers' perceptions of God in their own lives and in the lives of their listeners, making for more insightful and relevant homilies.

Today's World Calls for Honest Preaching

In a world inundated with words, the need for the preachers to preach the *Word* effectively has never been greater. At the same time, never before have preachers had to contend with what they do today. Every night people are exposed to television coverage of current affairs and subjects of human interest and concern. They see and hear professional presenters describing, discussing and assessing the rights and wrongs of various situations. This exposure has created a set of expectations with regard to people speaking in public, including preachers.

No industry knows the collective consciousness of a nation better than the media. It is alert to cultural norms and values and has worked hard at developing styles of presentation that use these to lend authority to what is said. It is into this world that the preacher has to bring the often counter-cultural values and attitudes of the gospel. No easy task!

For all its technological, medical, social and political sophistication, our modern world often leaves people with few answers to the questions of meaning in their lives. It was during the 1960s that young people brought these questions to the attention of our society. Today, they remain for many just as real and still unanswered. It is to this quest for authentic meaning that preachers are called to respond. It is their task to bring the truth of Christ to the questions of people.

In the present atmosphere it is critical that the preacher addresses these questions honestly. What does honest preaching involve?

People are accustomed to issues being analyzed and discussed. They are acutely aware of the complexity of the human endeavor. To oversimplify or to offer pious platitudes to such an audience will substantially undermine the credibility of the preacher and the preaching ministry. A simple way of protecting against this superficiality is to ask ourselves after each sentence of our homily, "Do I really believe that?"

Honest preaching is born out of honest preparation. Only when preachers have been prepared to struggle earnestly and rigorously with their matter are they likely to present homilies that contain insights considered of value by their listeners. Congregations today are much more discerning in their acceptance of preachers' opinions than was the case thirty years ago. To gain the confidence of their listeners, preachers need to be able to bring the gospel to them in a way that is fresh and invigorating. This requires more perspiration than inspiration.

No minister is more vulnerable to "ego inflation" than the preacher; and nothing is more obvious and off-putting to the listener. When we speak the Word of God often, it can happen that we begin to speak as God. "Ego inflation" is insidious and can happen despite the best intentions of the preacher. To insure against developing an arrogant attitude, preachers needs a trusted friend who is willing to remind them that they are not, nor do they need to be, God!

For all of its risks, honest preaching demands that preachers disclose their own stories of faith. Obviously, homilists need to guard against preaching their own agenda. Attending adequately to the story of the community and the story of the text will ensure this. At the same time, the text and the experience of the community need to be tested in the homilist's own experience. Without this, the homily risks sounding hollow and lacking conviction. In telling of personal experience, there are a couple of guidelines to keep in mind.

Firstly, make sure that the disclosure involved in the experience is appropriate for the audience. We would disclose things to a small prayer group of which we had been a member for a number of years that we would not disclose from the pulpit on Sunday. Discerning the appropriate level of disclosure is very important. If we over-disclose, we will embarrass our audience and distract them from the message of the homily. If we under-disclose, however, there is every chance the story will not have sufficient interest to capture them. Disclosure levels are worth discussing with our trusted friend.

Secondly, in relating our own experiences we need to develop the skill of speaking OUT OF the experience rather than simply *of* the experience. Experiences are told only to highlight the presence of God known within them. Stories told with this attitude will rarely come across as if the preacher is simply speaking about himself or herself. People then will become much better disposed to hear the whispers of God within the experience.

Vulnerability: The Essential Virtue for Ministry

We have stressed that like all ministry, preaching is about helping people experience the Kingdom announced by Jesus. Through the gospel stories we are shown how Jesus and others uncovered and responded to the Kingdom in their lives. In them is contained the fundamental paradigm for all ministry. Let us look first at the life of Jesus himself.

All of the Synoptics present the Baptism of Jesus as pivotal to his whole life and ministry. Their accounts clearly highlight the unique relationship Jesus felt with his God. While his experience of his God was, like yours and mine, grounded in his human experience, unlike you and me, his sinlessness allowed him to interpret this experience in a totally new way. The stories of the temptations in the desert after the Baptism sum up the pressure that Jesus must have felt to interpret his own experience of God according to the religious norms of the day. Despite these, he dared to be vulnerable to, and trust, his own experience, and to call God by a name that no Jew would ever use: "Abba".

Many of the stories we have that are grounded in the historical life of Jesus reflect this openness or vulnerability to his experience. It was in knowing his union with his Father that Jesus was empowered to carry out his mission of proclaiming and enacting the Kingdom.

While the stories of his life reflect Jesus' trust in the unconditional love of his Father, it is the story of his death that vindicates his trust. In a sense, his death challenged all he had lived for. Between them, the Synoptics present Jesus as beset by anxiety and even a hint of doubt. "Take this cup from me!". "Your will, not mine, be done!". "Into your hands I commend my Spirit": a triumphant cry, or a hopeful plea? In death Jesus trusted the Father as he had in life. His resurrection is the vindication of that trust. The Father who had supported him in life also supported him in death. He is absolutely faithful. At the heart of the life, death and resurrection of Jesus is this attitude of vulnerability.

In his ministry, Jesus invited and empowered people to live differently. Such was the radical nature of his message, however, that if people were to experience the freedom he offered they needed to become vulnerable to his message.

Take the centurion in the story of the healing of the servant in Lk. 7. He was a Roman with a pagan background. To allow himself firstly to be challenged by what Jesus said, and then to respond to and trust him in the way that he did, is a powerful statement of his willingness to be vulnerable to both the man and his message. In the gospel stories it is those who are able to be vulnerable to the message of Jesus who respond to his call. Those who assess what he says in terms of their own criteria, such as the Scribes and the Pharisees, are unable to hear his message.

Just as it was through vulnerability that the Kingdom became incarnate in the time of Jesus and the early Church, so it is today. A good example is Oscar Romero, the Archbishop in San Salvador. He was of the ruling class when appointed Archbishop. As he exposed himself and became vulnerable to the experience of his priests and people, he underwent a profound conversion which saw him spend his life fighting for justice, and which ultimately led to his death. Something of the Kingdom came into that part of the world, when a person became vulnerable to his own experience.

Our own faith experience is the same. When we are prepared to be vulnerable to our own religious experience and respond in love and trust, we taste the sweetness of the Father's love. When that happens the Kingdom becomes present. Vulnerability then, would seem to be the human precondition that facilitates the coming of the Kingdom.

It is in loving, and knowing the love of another, that we best experience the fruit of the virtue of vulnerability. If we reflect upon the relationships we have with those we love, it soon becomes clear that what makes the relationships special is that within them, not only do we share our strengths, but we are also able to share our weaknesses. In these relationships we take a risk and reveal to the other the inner secrets of our lives, trusting they will not use them to manipulate or destroy us. It is only in taking that risk that we know what it is to trust; and only when we know how to trust that we can come to know true love.

But to speak of the risk is to tell only half the story. What we find is that when we become vulnerable to another, it happens more often than not that our trust in them elicits from them a reciprocal trust in us. Our vulnerability to them encourages them to become vulnerable to us. It is from within this shared vulnerability that a bondedness begins to grow. True love happens when two people are prepared to become vulnerable to each other.

Developing Vulnerability Through Listening and Reflection

Developing and nurturing a way of life that disposes us to be vulnerable to our own experience and that of others is a lifelong task. In the development of this virtue, two things seem essential. Firstly, we need to listen to our own experience and the experience of others in a special way, and secondly, we need to develop a reflective lifestyle.

There are two different ways in which we can listen both literally and metaphorically, and the way we respond to what we hear will vary according to the way we listen. Firstly, we can listen *from the outside*. This is the style of listening normally used in our day-to-day interactions with people and events. We listen this way when we assess what we hear in the words and behavior of others, according to a personal set of criteria which we bring to the listening. When two people communicating are using this style of listening, *what* is said is like an object placed between them which both look at and assess according to their individual criteria.

Subsequent interchanges try to shape this object so that it is acceptable to the criteria of both. Usually, if the object cannot be shaped to the satisfaction of both, they simply agree to disagree. In more serious discussions, the original statement may be replaced by the criteria which each used to assess it. The criteria then become the object to be shaped, and so on.

When we listen this way, we tend to respond from the security of our own criteria and attempt to shape what we have heard according to them. Sometimes it may happen that we are forced to question our criteria, but this is more the exception than the rule. In a way our assessment criteria insulate us from having to change personally as the result of what we have heard.

The second style of listening and responding is very different. It involves *listening from within*. In this style we listen to the best of our ability to what others say *from their point of view*. Rather than assessing what is said according to our criteria, we become willing to allow the other point of view to challenge our criteria.

When we listen from the inside, our responses tend to be more a *searching with* the person to whom we are listening. The communication becomes a sharing of mutually gleaned insights. This style of listening is risky business, for it requires us to surrender our control over what we hear. It makes us personally vulnerable and may well cause us to challenge some of the "certainties" of our lives. Obviously, it is through listening from within that we become vulnerable to our own stories and those of others.

The development of a reflective lifestyle is the second way in which the virtue of vulnerability can be nourished.

There are a number of contrary but complementary aspects of life that contribute to its equilibrium. Each of them needs its own "time", and if we neglect one or the other, life tends to lose its balance. We need time to be awake and time to sleep; time to laugh and time to cry; time to work and time to play. As important as any of these is time to be present to our experience (to listen) and time to reflect.

Imagine your life and its experiences as a large room with a door opening into a corridor. When you wake you open the door and the experiences of life begin to present themselves. They may come through our external senses or our memory. You stand at the door and accept each experience and attend to the giver. As it passes you, you place it immediately behind you in your room. There is usually little time before the next experience is on the way and so there is little time to reflect upon each one. This goes on for as long as we are open to new experience. There comes a time when you need to close the door and begin to unpack some of them. They need to be sorted in terms of their meaning, and a decision made as to what is of value and what may be put aside. This attention to the inner world is reflection.

The balance between attention, or presence to new experience, and inner attention, or reflection, is so important. If we fail to attend to our experience, there is nothing to reflect upon. If on the other hand we fail to reflect, the door becomes so crowded that we are distracted from attending because of the pressure we feel from our unattended experiences.

Obviously we need time to close the door. In a cultural world obsessed with the material and the instant, and in which value is marked by productivity, it requires a firm decision and a strong commitment to give quality time to reflection. Christian ministers are called to bring the wisdom of the Kingdom to the experience of others. The level of human existence at which this dialogue occurs demands an appreciation of human experience that cannot be had without constant and serious reflection.

Just as we can listen *from the outside* and *from the inside*, so we can reflect *from the outside* and *from the inside*. The way we reflect upon an experience substantially affects the outcome of our reflection. Particular experiences call for the appropriate style of reflection. While everyone uses both styles, there is often a strong preference for reflecting *from the outside* which can restrict a more holistic appreciation of life.

We reflect *from the outside* when we try to isolate an experience, a situation or ourselves in order to analyze and understand. It is a *problem-solving* style of reflection that aims at gaining some kind of control over the experience through understanding. An image may help.

Sometimes a play begins with a spotlight on the leading actor and actress. The background remains in darkness and all of our attention is directed towards that which is spotlighted. In the same way, reflecting upon experience from the outside brings it under the scrutiny of the white light of reason.

This style of reflection is encouraged within our Western culture which has an obvious bias in favor of cause and effect, rational types of thinking. It is an essential part of balanced human living. Without understanding, and the integration that comes from it, we become buffeted by one experience after another. Soon life can begin to lead us, rather than we leading our life.

But this style of reflection also has its limitations. When understanding and integration are not readily achieved, we can become prone to view the whole of life through one part. This is not a bad lay person's definition of neurosis. Excessive reflection upon experience from the outside, especially negative experience, can lead to an obsession with that particular aspect of our lives and this can become completely debilitating. How often in our ministry have we seen people become so obsessed with a "failure" in one small aspect of their lives which leads them to see all of it as a failure.

Reflecting exclusively in this way can lead to categorical thinking. When we direct our analytical mind to an experience in order to understand it, we do so using a set of ideals of behavior and thought that we have developed over the years. Since these are ideals, we find that our actual behavior often comes up short. As a result, we can become "tyrannized by the oughts and the shoulds" in our lives, with the consequent feelings of guilt and remorse. As well, this style of reflection may dispose us towards a preoccupation with our own opinion. We become so caught up in our own understanding of experience that we filter out any alternative interpretation.

Reflection from the outside tends to *look at* experiences. By emphasizing the objectivity of the experiences, it can cause people to feel a separation between themselves and their experience. This characteristic of the style becomes a problem when used excessively in reflecting upon interpersonal relationships. It can predispose people to think of others more as objects than as people with whom they are in relationship.

Along with this tendency to objectify, the heavy emphasis the style places on understanding can blind us to the deeper mysteries of life. There are certain experiences in life that go beyond our understanding and over which we have little control. Birth and death, love and hate would be in this category, and so are those experiences of Mystery that break in upon us in the midst of our ordinary human experience. Because in reflection from the outside there is little room for surprise, it can happen that we are blinded to our experience of the God of surprises.

Developing our capacity to reflect *from the inside* complements that of reflecting *from the outside* and protects us from its excesses. In terms of the image of the actors on stage, reflecting from the inside is possible when the lights of the set are turned up and we can see the actors in their total context. In reflecting from the inside we use our imaginations to recreate the experience and then "walk within" it and "re-feel" it, alert to our relationship to it and its various aspects.

It is this interest in the relational aspects of life that characterizes this style of reflection. It has a keen eye for noticing how a person is related to their inner world, to other people, and to creation. Attention to this aspect develops within us a sense of bondedness with life. Since relationships are in a state of constant flux, this style encourages us to be sensitive to the dynamic nature of life. It disposes us to let go of any need to control and manipulate the meaning of the experience, allowing us to involve ourselves fully in the ebb and flow of life.

As well, it best prepares us to hear the presence of God in the midst of our ordinary human experience. By encouraging an appreciation of the interconnectedness of life, we are predisposed to wonder at its beauty and mystery. This attitude helps us to perceive experiences in which God breaks in on our lives. As has already been said, such religious experience primarily discloses more about our relationship with, rather than the nature of, God. Inside reflection, with its sensitivity to relationships, helps us to be aware of the full significance of these revelatory experiences.

Like the two styles of listening, the two styles of reflecting resemble the black and white keys of a piano. When we learn to play them appropriately together, we will begin to experience the full beauty of the music of life.

The Christian tradition has long recognized the need for reflection in its common practices. Times for prayer and reading, involvement in ritual and the periodic undertaking of retreats are taken for granted as part and parcel of Christian living. In addition to these, having set aside quality time, there are a number of helpful vehicles that can assist with both styles of reflection.

For reflection upon the more intimate areas of our inner life, it is most helpful to have a trusted friend. By sharing our experiences with this person, we are given the opportunity to own them in a relationship of trust. In taking a "second look" at experiences we will often hear in them much more than was perceived in the immediacy of the experience itself. We may well become aware of some of the unconscious filters operating in our lives, and so have the opportunity to accept or reject them. While having a chat with this friend may well become a social occasion, it helps if the meeting also involves some structured time of sharing.

Faith sharing and prayer groups present another helpful way in which we are encouraged to reflect upon our lives. These are most helpful when they focus more on sharing than discussion. It is amazing how much insight is gained by telling our own stories and by listening, from the inside, to others telling theirs.

While at times demanding, a most helpful tool can be journal writing. In a journal we describe our significant experiences, including the moods, feelings and reactions that accompany them, in a non-judgmental way. The more we practice the method the more we are able to "unpack" our feelings. Instead of being sad we might describe ourselves as being brooding, morose, weepy, fragile, etc.

The journal always needs to stay in touch with the original experience and, in line with inside reflection, needs to remain faithful to its context and as free as possible from personal bias. Again this becomes easier as we practice. The journal will often allow us to see the patterns of our behavior and responses, and the biases they carry.

Finally, journaling will occasionally provide us with glimpses of our unconscious. If we are able to write from within the experience, it will sometimes happen that through the images and symbols in the writing we will be made aware of the needs of our unconscious, and how it is manifesting itself in our conscious lives.

Reflection Through Images

Much of life's significant experience, including our experience of God, is perceived through the imagination. Reflecting upon experience through images often yields aspects of meaning not readily available through conscious scrutiny.

Once we have examined our experience as well as we can, using the guidelines above, it is always helpful to ask "What is it like?". When an image surfaces, listen to it from the inside and see what it may disclose about itself. Take these insights and look at the original experience through them.

Two exercises that I and others have found helpful, are to write your life story, firstly as a river, and secondly, as a garden. In the writing be sure to stay within the metaphor. For example, a peaceful time may be described like this:

> "Gradually the high banks gave way to lower banks and I could see they were free of the gouging of flood waters. No longer did I feel the constriction of the banks. While they still provided my limits, I accepted them without a fight and felt comfortable with them. I could see the countryside for miles, which was refreshing having previously spent so much time looking only at my own banks. It was lush with grass and dotted with trees. I appreciated the beauty of my world and was grateful that I had something to contribute to this beauty. I met some new friends at that stage. Some came to be nourished. They drank my water and enjoyed its purity and coolness for at that stage my water ran deep. Others came to play and to fish and just enjoy my company."

Once the writing about a particular period has been completed, enter the images again and feel them from the inside. Through the insights that emerge, remember the experiences of that time in your conscious memory and see if you understand them differently.

Listening to and reflecting upon our life's experience helps us develop the virtue of vulnerability. No virtue stands homilists in better stead for their ministry.

Attending to the Preacher's Experience

Finally, in the actual preparation stage, the homilist needs to give some attention to his or her own experience over the last week or so.

What have been the significant experiences: in the world, the community, personally?

How have they affected me?

Are there personal issues that are likely to affect the homily?

Have I experienced God in these experiences? How?

How has my faith influenced my response?

If no issues of faith have been raised, why not?

Has anything happened to cause me to doubt or change my faith?

In addition to these questions, the methods suggested in Chapter 7 on community are also suitable for teasing out the experience of the preacher. Nothing contributes more to good preaching than a lively faith. There is truth in the old adage, "Good preachers preach because they have something to say, not because they have to say something!"

SECTION
FOUR

Producing
the Homily

Preparing and Delivering the Homily

I HAPPENED TO BE stationed at the Cathedral in Toowoomba during the golden jubilee celebrations of our diocese. The Cardinal Archbishop of Sydney, James Freeman, was invited to give the homily at the Jubilee Mass. After the ceremony, the local press asked for a copy of the homily. I had noticed that he had not taken any notes into the pulpit, but decided to ask him anyhow. "Certainly", he said. "If you go over to my room you will find a copy of the text on top of my briefcase." He knew the text by heart!

Good homilies happen when homilists take the time to adequately prepare them. Fail to prepare and be prepared to fail! All homiletic theory can do is present guidelines that will assist homilists to maximize the effect of their efforts.

The time ministers are prepared to give to homily preparation will depend to a large extent upon the importance they place on the ministry. I believe it is the most significant pastoral tool the parish minister possesses.

Since the Vatican Council, there has been a good deal of talk within the religious orders of the Catholic tradition about the "Order's Charism". Many of the orders have searched their beginnings to rediscover the distinctive spirit of their founders, with a view to reshaping their present ministries accordingly.

If we were to ask what is the distinctive charism required for parish ministry, we might well respond that it is the call to uncover for people the presence of God in the ordinariness of their lives. There are times when we all need the invaluable assistance of a specialist in the development of our relationship with God. However, most of us, for most of the time, live fairly ordinary lives.

Parish ministers are the ones who stand with us in this ordinariness. They were there with our parents to welcome us into the world and the Church and they were there to welcome our children into the world and the Church; they were there to celebrate our marriages and they are there to celebrate our children's marriages; they were there to farewell our parents and console us and they will be there to farewell us and console our children. Theirs certainly is a ministry to the magnificent ordinariness of simply living and dying.

This is the context of the Sunday homily. For most Christians, it will provide the only specifically Christian reflection upon their experience they will make for the week. It may well be the only means through which they may come to know the loving presence of God in their lives. It will probably be the only way in which they will be challenged to facilitate the coming of the Kingdom in their world. There will be more acute opportunities for ministries during the week, and these are important and demand the minister's attention. But for the majority, the Sunday homily will be the only care they will receive from their minister that week. It is difficult to understand how a pastor can really care and yet not adequately prepare the Sunday homily.

The Four Stages of Preparation

Homily preparation takes time, not only in terms of the actual hours spent directly researching, reflecting and writing, but also as a process. Preaching is an art form born out of the creative process at work within the homilist. Creative ideas are spawned in the unconscious and born into our conscious minds.

Integral to this process is a natural ebb and flow. It needs some time for intense conscious concentration, and for relaxation when the unconscious is able to deliver its insights. Then it needs concentration and effort to shape the insight in a meaningful way for an audience. Finally, it needs time to appreciate the beauty and meaning of the insight. Unless the process includes time for each of these phases it becomes crippled. In order to give it the time it requires the homilist needs to begin preparation early in the week.

There are several specific stages in the preparation process that can be identified.

A. Searching the Sources

Preparation usually begins by searching the sources and gathering ideas. This is an intense stage requiring homilists to attend to the text, the community and their own lives. Out of both respect and habit most begin by attending to the text. My experience is that it is better to attend to the community first, then our own lives, and the text last. This way we can begin to view human experience through the text which makes for a better dialogue between the text and life. Whichever pole we begin with, it is essential that *all three* be addressed.

It is better to attend to each of the poles separately in three shorter sittings, than to all three in the one sitting. This way each pole has a better chance of disclosing its interests and concerns. There is included at the end of the methods for addressing each pole in Chapters 6, 7, and 8, a reflective process that brings Scripture and experience into dialogue. It is important to use this as the ideas emerge from each of the poles. Often the Scripture that comes to mind from an exegesis of the experience of both the community and the homilist may not include the set text of the homily. Reciprocally, the experiences triggered by the text may not be the present experience of the community or the homilist. Usually, however, there are some connecting threads that become obvious.

Using this dialogical process encourages what educationalists call "selective perception". An example probably describes its meaning best:

There was a restaurant in Kensington named the Paragon. I suggested to a friend that we eat there one evening. He commented upon the name and said how popular it was for country cafes. Until he pointed that out I had never noticed. Since then however, I have been amazed at how many country towns have a Paragon cafe. I seem to notice them now without even looking.

"Selective perception" can often help to focus the interrelated ideas contained in the various sources. Allow as many ideas as possible to surface. Jot each of them down without making judgment on their relative merits. At this stage quantity breeds quality.

Once all three poles have been attended to, and all ideas collected, sort them into two groups: problems and solutions. Analyze each of the ideas by asking some of the relevant questions outlined in Chapters 6, 7, and 8 on the sources. For those ideas that are problems, begin to think of possible solutions, and vice versa. Be particularly alert to any discrepancies you notice between the gospel insights and attitudes and values operating within individuals and the community. Note as well any correspondence in the lists between problems and solutions.

There are a couple of very important criteria to keep in the back of the mind at this stage. In attending to the sources, homilists are seeking an insight that will make a difference in the lives of their listeners. Beware of the temptation to get caught up in the intrigue of an insight into humanity or theology; that may be intellectually fascinating both for the preacher and his or her audience, but will have little impact upon the way people interpret and live their lives. Remember, homilies are about changing attitudes and behavior.

It has been stressed throughout that the homily attempts to bring the light of the gospel to that partly conscious and largely unconscious assumptive world of people: the world from which attitudes and values develop. As we list ideas that come from the various sources, we need to have an eye for those insights that address this world. While it is in specific behavior that this world manifests itself, homilists need to be on their guard against using insights that simply address the behavior without attending to the deeper assumptive world.

Without prematurely discarding any ideas that may have come from the various sources, even at this early stage it is helpful for the homilist to have these filters in place. With experience, of course, they begin to operate automatically.

Finally, pick out a few people from the congregation that will hear the homily. From your knowledge of their background and interests, put yourself in their place and ask yourself how they would respond to the ideas in the lists. Make sure you choose people with different backgrounds and interests and that you pick different people each week.

Allowing Ideas to Simmer and Distil Their Insights

Once the intense work of searching the sources for ideas and insights has been completed, it is time to leave them aside for a while and allow them to "simmer in their own juice". This pause is integral to the creative process. It allows interaction between the ideas without the restriction of conscious attention.

It can happen that after all the work done in addressing the various sources, homilists feel they are without a preachable insight. Do not be discouraged. Be assured, if the work has been done in the first stage, this gestation will result in an insight that can be shaped into a meaningful homily. Naturally, some will be better than others, but rarely will it happen that some meaningful insight does not surface.

This gestation period tends to distil its insights into consciousness at times when our thinking processes are not the center of our attention. There is no better illustration of this than the story of Archimedes. His king was suspicious of the royal crown maker whom he suspected of making his crowns from an amalgam of silver and gold. He gave Archimedes the task of discovering whether the crown maker was honest. If he could not discover a way to do this, he was to be executed. Archimedes struggled with the problem, but all to no avail. Exhausted, he decided a solution was beyond him and went home and ran a bath. The furthest thing from his mind when he stepped into the bath was a solution to his problem. But that was the moment the solution struck him. He realized that because of their different consistencies, a piece of silver or gold weighing the same would displace a different quantity of water. This way he could establish whether it was gold or an amalgam being used by the crown maker. As the story goes, he ran naked through the streets shouting "Eureka!".

Most preachers are also parish ministers, and this story highlights an aspect of their lifestyle that warrants some consideration. Parish ministers today tend to do a lot more talking about emotional and spiritual wounds than binding up physical wounds. Such a concentration upon our thinking capacity can prove an impediment to the creative capacity of the minister. The creative process calls for a balance between intense mental activity and an involvement in physical activities. More often than not it is during these periods, when the thinking capacity of the person is not engaged, that the unconscious will disclose significant insights.

In addition to the "Archimedes' bath" situations that are part and parcel of life, there are many ways in which ministers can engage in some sort of physical activity. For some it may be sport; for others, the garden. In view of the creative nature of their ministry, preachers need to give consideration to their lifestyle. If a minister is having difficulty in discovering meaningful insights for his or her homily, rather than increase the time of thinking, involvement in some kind of physical activity may need to be increased. Preachers will be pleasantly surprised at how many insights come to them during these periods.

I can remember someone saying once that the reason why there is less mental illness in country areas is simply because country people work more with their hands; being in touch with the soil helps to keep people anchored within life. I believe this is correct. A balanced lifestyle not only makes for better homilies, but more contented homilists.

By the end of this process one or two insights will begin to dominate. This is the time for decisions. Preachers have to make a pastoral judgment on which they intend to use. While it is a time for choosing, it is also a time for letting go. Often a preacher will be tempted to share two or three insights that have surfaced. While each may have its merit, only one should be chosen. To communicate one insight effectively within a ceremony of worship is sufficiently demanding for both preachers and their congregations. Too many potentially good homilies have been spoiled because the preacher lacked the discipline to deal with just one insight.

The insights discarded are never lost. I have been amazed at how often an unpreached insight has proven most valuable in another aspect of ministry during the same week.

Once we have decided upon the insight we wish to use, we are ready to begin shaping it through writing.

Writing a Draft

The homily addresses those areas of people's lives that create and maintain meaning. In these the imagination has a key role. Appropriately then, not only should homilists keep this in mind when choosing their content and language, but also when they choose the structure to develop their homily.

One of the languages of the imagination is story. What attracts the attention of the imagination is not only the content of stories, but also their form. And it is this form that can provide a most appropriate and very effective outline for the development of the homily.

Eugene Lowry was the originator of this homiletical style in his book *The Homiletical Plot*. Since first reading the book I have encouraged many students to adopt the style. While it has taken some time and practice, in the main it has produced for them very effective homilies.

This is not to say there will not be occasions in worship when a more didactic style would be appropriate. These, however, would be the exception rather than the rule. Over the long haul narrative form is more likely to produce a consistently effective homily.

Developing a Homily According to Narrative Form

At the heart of all stories is their *plot*. Through the plot readers are first taken in their imagination into a situation in which there is conflict requiring some kind of resolution. As the story unfolds, the conflict is gradually resolved. It is the felt need for resolution that maintains a reader's interest.

According to this form, Lowry suggests that a homily could be developed through five stages:

Upsetting the equilibrium;
Analyzing the discrepancy;
Disclosing the clue to the resolution;
Experiencing the gospel;
Anticipating the consequences.

What follows is a method of preparation based loosely upon this form, with one significant variation. One of the most distinctive aspects of the form Lowry suggests is that the clue to the resolution of the ambiguity will not come from where we expect. This is based upon a theological position that stresses the discontinuity between the wisdom of the world and the wisdom of God contained in the gospel. Lowry suggests that the analysis be done from the point of view of worldly wisdom, so that when the clue to resolution contained in the gospel is disclosed it will come as a surprise to the listener.

While I agree with his observation about discontinuity, I would not wish to stress it. Indeed, I would be keen to encourage people to hear the whispers of the gospel within their own experience. My experience has been that by allowing an "analyzed ambiguity" to directly interact with a "reflected upon" text, listeners are surprised by the insights they receive, and upon which they are able to act.

In terms of preparation, I would suggest combining the disclosure of the clue with the experiencing of the gospel.

With this form in the back of our mind, we are ready to begin a draft.

A thorough search of the sources, and the period of gestation yield the insight to be developed in the homily. As well, they often produce some ideas as to how that insight could be developed. These are important. However, it is just as important not to become too enamored of them. Just as good writers listen to their characters as they develop in a novel, so good homilists can listen to the insight as it develops in the writing. The development of an insight through the writing of a draft will often be very different to what the homilist may have expected. In a sense, homilists need to allow the insight to write itself. It is their task to simply shape it for the circumstances in which it will be preached.

As well, they need to remember that the homily is being prepared to be spoken. The spoken word has a different rhythm to the written. Speaking aloud each phrase and sentence as it is written in the draft, will minimize the polishing needed before it is actually delivered.

1. Engaging the Audience

The opening of a homily aims to capture the attention of the congregation. It needs to be sufficiently arresting to shake people free of their preoccupying thoughts, and entice them to reflect on a particular aspect of their personal or community life which will eventually be brought to the gaze of the gospel. The homily is like a vehicle taking people on a journey into their own lives. While in one sense the homilist is the driver, the direction of the journey will largely depend on the life experience of the listeners and the community. The homilist needs to keep in mind that the homily is simply a means through which people visit aspects of their lives and discover there the presence of God.

The first task is to encourage people to get into the vehicle! This is best done by uncovering for them an aspect of their lives that is ambiguous. Lowry expresses it so clearly by saying we begin by alerting people to an "itch" in their lives that needs "scratching". While the initial insight gained in the earlier stages of preparation may have come in the form of a solution, the homily always begins by describing the problem. Always describe the "itch" before you offer the "scratch".

One of the easiest and most effective ways to engage the

attention of people is to tell a story. The selection is very important. Appropriate experiential stories will often come out of
reflection upon the sources. There are any number of books
available with a wide range of fictional stories suitable for homilies. Movies, television, novels are all rich sources. The story needs
to be one which listeners can enter easily. Try to choose a story that
not only points to the problem, but also includes at least a
suggestion of the solution. It should not be a re-telling of the
gospel.

A story is used at this stage to focus attention on an aspect of
people's lives in an attempt to help them feel some kind of a
discrepancy between how they are living and how they would like
to be living. It is this felt ambiguity that initially engages, and then
continues to hold the interest of an audience. If this is achieved, the
psyche's natural urge to overcome ambiguity begins to work for
the homily.

When selecting a story, the homilist needs to keep in mind its
power. It can happen that the initial story of a homily is so
powerful that it captures the listeners and will not release them to
hear the remainder of the homily. So a story needs to be selected
which will engage people, but also release them.

If a very powerful story seems appropriate, like the story of the
bag-lady, it is probably better to use it as a parable in its own right
and not as part of a homily.

While a story is probably the easiest way to engage an audience,
it is not the only way. Certainly I am not suggesting that every
homily should begin with a story. An arresting statement can do
the same thing. Something like "Life is what happens when you've
made other plans!", followed by a general description of the truth
of the statement, would capture an audience as successfully as a
story. The homily's opening aims at highlighting an ambiguous
aspect of people's lives. This is what is paramount. Use of a story is
simply a means to achieving this aim.

2. Highlighting and Analyzing the Discrepancy

Once people begin to feel the ambiguity, it is important that it not
be resolved too quickly. It is a little like bringing wood to a fire. A
person has to pick it up and walk with it for a way before
discarding it onto the fire and benefiting from its heat. Once
homilists arouse interest in the ambiguity of an aspect of someone's

life, they need to assist the person to walk with that ambiguity, feel it, and understand it. To suggest its resolution too quickly will lessen the impact of the new awareness. People are more likely to change after they themselves have struggled with an aspect of their lives and reached some sort of personal resolution, than as the result of another's suggestion.

This is the stage of analysis within the homily, and it is the stage that is so often omitted. Here the listener is encouraged to ask *why?* Why is this ambiguity in our lives? What are the assumptions, attitudes and values underpinning present behavior? All the research and reflection done earlier provides the content for this stage. The homilists lead their listeners along some of the paths they themselves have trodden while addressing the text, the community, and their own lives.

This is the inquiry stage for the audience and homilists need to concentrate on helping them ask questions, rather than sharing with them some of the answers they may have deduced when they asked themselves the questions. In terms of the vehicle image, the homilist ferries people around the particular ambiguity within their lives, helping them to see it from a number of different aspects. The ferrying is more important than sharing the fruit of their own inquiries.

Be careful that this section does remain a genuine inquiry section. There can be a temptation to substitute an analysis of the ambiguity with a number of different illustrations of it. This diminishes the insightfulness of the homily.

By doing this section well, homilists manifest their sensitivity to the complexity of life. It is this section that ensures the homily remains in the world of the listeners and does not fall prey to the tyranny of generalization.

3. Experiencing the Gospel

Once the ambiguity has been explored, it is time to begin moving towards a resolution. Again, this initially is a stage of exploration and discovery for the listeners. The homilist draws their attention to the text and shares something of his or her own research and reflection. Give only enough exegesis to highlight the gospel insights relevant to the resolution of the ambiguity. It is important that at this stage the listeners are assisted to *look through* the text at their lives. If too much exegesis is given, they can become more interested in the text itself rather than how it interprets this particular ambiguous aspect of their lives.

In this section, homilists may choose to share something of how the text helped them resolve the ambiguity in their lives. If so, they need to be careful not to present this as the *only* way in which the text may resolve the ambiguity. The Spirit blows where it wills and can never be contained in the insights of one person.

Timing is all important to this stage. It is like telling a good joke. The punch line needs to be delivered at exactly the right moment for it to be most effective. The clues of the gospel need to be delivered after a significant search but before people lose interest. Experience with the method will help develop this sense of timing. *Bringing the ambiguous human experience under the gaze of the text is the high point of the homily.*

4. Anticipating the Consequences

The last stage is to explore the consequences of the insight that the interaction yielded. If the homilist has managed to create a significant interaction between people's experience and the gospel message, then he or she will have tapped a source of motivation in their listeners' lives that will empower them to change.

Within all authentic religious experience is contained an imperative and an empowerment. The experience calls people to change, but it also empowers them to respond to the call. Consequently, this section of the homily is not so much concerned with exhorting and motivating people to act differently — that is the work of the Spirit. At this stage homilists simply try to suggest ways in which people may shape their own personal responses. As in the last section, they may share something of what they see themselves called to or what they see the community called to. Again they need to present these as *their* way of responding and not the *only* way.

5. Disposing People for Eucharist

Finally, the conclusion should make for a smooth transition into the next stage of the worship. If the homily has been effective, people will now want to celebrate their new awareness of the presence of God in their lives.

Once the draft has been completed, set it aside for a period. It too needs some time to "stew in its own juice". While normally the draft will not be changed substantially, sometimes this period will help to discover a way of treating a section of the homily that may have presented difficulties during drafting.

The last stage of the whole process is to polish the draft for delivery.

Firstly, it is always advisable to check the accuracy of the theological assumptions contained in the text.

Then look to the style of the homily. The important criterion here is to ask "How does it sound to the ears of the listeners?" It is best to speak the homily out aloud. Listen to it through the ears of the congregation. Short, sharp phrases and sentences sound best.

Make sure the words used are easily understood. Replace any technical theological language that may be misunderstood. Remember that most listeners will have read very little theology, and even the most simple theological terms may prove confusing.

Delete generalizations and make sure any stories or illustrations used are graphically phrased and easy to visualize for the listener.

Check the rhythm and the timing of the various sections.

Ensure there is a smooth development of the plot and that the tension is held throughout.

There is a great deal of satisfaction to be gained from the preparation of a good homily. While the homily attempts to facilitate an experience of God for the listener, the preparation often facilitates this for the homilist.

Once the homily is ready for delivery, always take the time to savor the fruit of your labor. Homiletics is an art form and the artist is entitled, and indeed needs, to enjoy the beauty of his or her creation. While the affirmation of listeners is invaluable for the preacher, there is no substitute for knowing that you will preach not because you have to say something, but because you have something of value to say.

Delivering the Homily

While the following suggestions are restricted to the delivery of the homily, it must be remembered that as most preachers are also presidents of worship, the delivery manner they adopt for homilies will be closely linked to their style of presidency. Attitudes have more influence here than is often recognized. It will quickly become clear to a community whether a preacher/president feels he or she is worshiping *with* them or conducting the worship *for* them. The tone of voice used and the personal manner adopted by the president/preacher will be largely influenced by the way he or she sees the ministry.

Reciprocally for the ministers, by examining some of the characteristics of their presidential style and delivery manner and tone, they are able to uncover their real attitudes.

While the homily should always be written, it should *never* be read! Much of the value of the work of preparation is lost if a preacher reads the homily. Some find it helpful to make a set of notes from the draft, containing the significant stages of development and the phrases that mark each stage. Others take the full text with them, but only refer to it as they would to notes. Those gifted with good memories, like Cardinal Freeman, may not need to take anything. Experimentation is needed to find out which works best for each individual.

Become aware of gestures used, or as is more often the case, gestures not used. Check to see if they are appropriate in the eyes of the listeners. Much of what is said can be affirmed or undermined by gestures. As well, check with some community members about your personal mannerisms to see if they distract. Since these are usually unconscious, preachers will only become aware of them when someone points them out. I heard a man say once that his preacher rocked back and forth so much during his homilies that he almost became seasick!

Videotaping is used extensively to address this aspect of delivery in preparing preachers today. On some occasions, such as weddings, parish ministers are videoed. Much can be learned by looking critically at the tape.

It is easier to check the vocal delivery. Tape some homilies to see what your preaching voice sounds like. While the tone of public delivery will always vary from that of conversational speech, some will notice that their "presidential/preaching voice" is very different from their conversational voice. As I indicated earlier, this *may* indicate to them something about how they envisage their ministry. If the discrepancy is too great, it can sound hollow to the ears of the listeners and distract from the homily.

From taping it is also possible to pick up the rhythm and tone of delivery. Be alert to detecting patterns of delivery that may distract. For example, some preachers will use the one tone and rhythm of voice to mark the end of stages in the homily. As a result, they develop a lilt in their delivery which can become quite distracting.

Learn the vagaries of the sound system being used. Unfortunately many churches have inadequate sound systems and the impact of many good homilies suffers as a result. By taping homilies, and asking for accurate feedback from listeners, it is possible to find out appropriate levels of volume.

It is a marvelous privilege to be called to the ministry of preaching. This is a ministry of great trust. God trusts preachers with His Word, and people trust them to bring this Word to make meaning of their inner lives. Significant decisions in people's lives are made under the influence of the ministry of preaching. While many feel there is no more satisfying, fulfilling and inspiring ministry within parish life than preaching, most also feel humbled by its challenges.

If any ministry is collaborative, preaching must surely be it. It involves preachers collaborating with God, with people, and with their own inner lives in developing and appreciating the presence of God in our lives and in our world. I, and others, have found the following prayer helpful in disposing us to deliver a homily:

"Lord help me to say what You want me to say,
So that people will hear what You want them to
hear!"

Using the Method: A Sample Homily

THE FOLLOWING is an outline of how the suggested method may be used to prepare a homily. The readings are from the Catholic Lectionary for the thirtieth Sunday in Ordinary time, Year A: Ex. 22,20–26; Ps. 17:2–4,17,51; Thes. 1,5–10; Mt. 22,34–40. The setting for the homily is a middle-class Sydney parish. Obviously the content is conditioned by what is happening in the world, Australia, Sydney and the parish at present.

My aim here is not so much to produce an ideal homily, as to show how the method can be used within the time available in a busy parish schedule to produce an effective one. The following homily took between four and five hours to produce over three days. Might I add that the preparation time had benefits beyond the actual homily produced.

A. Searching the Sources:

The following are the notes that I jotted down while reflecting upon the various sources:

1. The Community

a. INTERNATIONAL EVENTS
   Kurdish situation in Iraq:
       the human misery of an oppressed people;
       no homeland;
       the wages of sectarianism?

oppression often comes from individuals seeking personal power;

paradox of international law:

U.N. prepared to back the liberation of Kuwait but will not interfere in the "internal" affairs of a nation. Is this justice?

The complexity of international politics.

Where is the Kingdom in all of this?

b. NATIONAL

The public inquiry into the Western Australian government;

The credibility of politicians;

The importance of public life and the contribution we need to make;

The impact of the recession: sense of uncertainty about the future; unemployment.

c. LOCAL

Continuing violence: murders, bashings, etc.

State elections.

d. PARISH

Good "feel" in the parish from the PARISH 2000 program (current parish renewal program)

Growing involvement of people.

2. Personal

Visit from friends;

Importance of friendship and its satisfactions;

The demands of relationships;

The experience of the love between Bill and Evelyn.

3. Text

a. THE EXEGESIS

i.   Textual variations: "Lawyer" for "One of them" in vs. 35.

ii. Specific references: Sadducees; Pharisees; "Law and prophets".

iii. Significant words, phrases: "to disconcert him", vs. 35.

iv. Themes: Wholehearted love of God and neighbor;
The equating of these;
The relationship and interaction between law and people;
The controversy between Jesus and the Pharisees and Sadducees;
The "fulfillment theme": Jesus is the fulfillment of the Law and the prophets.

v. Context: Follows passage on resurrection in which Jesus clashes with Sadducees;
One of five "clashes" with Judaism as Jesus moves towards Jerusalem and his death.

vi. Evangelist portraying Jesus as the fulfillment of the Law;
This is important for Mt's largely Jewish audience.

vii. Paraphrase: When the Pharisees heard that Jesus had made a deep impression on people in the way that he had handled the question put to him by the Sadducees, they were keen to undermine his influence.

So one of them, speaking the mind of the group, said to him, "Teacher, what is the greatest commandment of the Law?". Jesus said, "You must love the Lord your God wholeheartedly. This can only be done when you also love your neighbor wholeheartedly. The one includes the other. This is what the Law and the prophets is really all about!".

viii. Commentaries stress that the way in which Jesus elevated the love of neighbor to the same importance as the love of God is unique.

b. USING THE EXEGESIS

i. By listening as a member of Mt's community, i.e. through Jewish Christian ears:
The struggle and challenge to let go of a way of living that has been shaped through the observance of specific laws.

The challenge to love others is a challenge to creatively respond to life, as we experience it, rather than just from community expectation.

ii. From the cultural setting of the text in Jesus' time: the elevation of love of neighbor to the level of love of God is original.

Notice how the Pharisees align themselves with a traditional foe, the Sadducees, in trying to put Jesus down. The self-interest of groups and people will work together against goodness!

iii. From the Pharisees' point of view: A feeling of embarrassment and deflation at the authority of Jesus' tone.

A feeling of being challenged to rethink as a result of the question. From challenging to being challenged.

B. The Insight

From the concentrated reflection, a few insights arose:

i. The struggle people have to be released from the tyranny of law. This seemed to come mainly from the text.

ii. How personal interests and a desire for power prevent true love. This came from the situation in Iraq at the time, but resonated with the Pharisees in the text.

The challenge to love others and why it is so difficult. While this is part of the message of the text, it also resonated with my own experience of the last week or so, as well as some of the things happening in the world and community at this time. This was the insight I chose to use.

C. A Draft of the Homily

I have included headings to show the structural plan of the homily.

1. Engaging the Audience

Some years ago I was working at the St Vincent de Paul Hostel in Brisbane. Part of the ministry involved visiting the detox unit at the

Royal Brisbane Hospital. One afternoon I spent some time with a man by the name of Bill. We got on well right from the start. He was a Catholic and when I mentioned I was a priest it made the conversation even easier. He was a smallish man with a bit of a hunch in his back. He smoked constantly and there was a rasp in his voice that had come from drinking two bottles of methylated spirits a day for the last week or so. He had tried many times to get sober.

I'll never forget his voice nor his eyes that afternoon. His eyes filled with tears as he spoke of what he'd done to his wife and family. There was a genuineness in his voice that almost brought tears to my eyes as I listened to him. But for all the remorse there was little hope. He was almost at the stage of absolute despair.

I had little to offer except to encourage him to come to an A.A. meeting.

I went back the next day to visit Bill. This time Evelyn, his wife, was with him. They were sitting quietly on a bench outside the ward. I sat with them for a little while and eventually both Bill and Evelyn began to talk about the problems the disease had brought into their home. It was a drinking story that spread over twenty years and was filled with all the things that happen in a family ravished by this disease.

At one stage, Bill held his head in his hands and shakily said he thought it might be best if Evelyn left him. He didn't want to hurt her any more.

Without even as much as a pause Evelyn put her arm around him and said to him: "We've been through some bad times in the past and we've got through. There may be some bad times in the future. But somehow together we'll manage!"

That afternoon I glimpsed true love; and I was profoundly moved.

2. Highlighting and Analyzing the Discrepancy

Love really is what life is all about, so why is it that we find it so hard to love and be loved?

Sometimes we reach our hand out in love towards someone only to draw it back sometimes burned, sometimes bruised or broken. Maybe it's those hurtful experiences lodged deep in our memories that make us wary in love. Maybe they are the cause of our insulating ourselves against the possible hurt we may experience in loving another.

If this is the case, it would seem they are costing us dearly!

In many ways, loving plays havoc with personal interests and freedom. To love involves looking to the needs of another rather than concentrating upon our own personal interests.

Like most I was moved and at times shocked by the television reports of what happened to the Kurdish people in northern Iraq. No doubt it was a complex political and religious situation, but what was happening there has been influenced by the lust for power of one man. What was being played out on our television screens before our eyes, was a reflection of something that may well be happening in our lives.

Within us all there is, if not a lust, at least a strong desire to have our own way. It is this often unconscious inner urge that prevents us from loving. Sometimes to love another appears to have little in it for us and so is not worth the trouble.

A friend once said to me, "It really takes time to be friends!" How simple, and yet how profound! Friendship and love do take time, and time is not something most of us have a lot of in our busy world. So much of our time is caught up in getting, that there is little available for giving. It is not that we plan things that way; it is just the way things seem to be. The pace of our lives may well be the very thing making it hard for us to love.

3. Experiencing the Gospel

"Love God wholeheartedly through loving your neighbor" is Jesus' reply to the Pharisee. Maybe that was what Evelyn was really saying when she said, "We have managed in the past!"

There is something special in loving another and being loved in return. It goes beyond the circumstances of the situation. In love we come to know the bigger picture of life. In love, despite the fact that the odds may seem to be stacked against us, we somehow know that all will be O.K.

One thing the gospel is saying to us today is that when we love another we love God. In a song from the musical *Les Miserables* we hear the words, "To love another person is to see the face of God". That seems to be another way of expressing one of the truths that Jesus is disclosing in today's gospel.

4. Anticipating the Consequences

Maybe this morning we are being called to pause and reflect upon the loves of our lives.

To feel again that "something special" at the heart of our
relationship with the people we love.
Maybe to see that it is here, at the very core of our being,
that God is truly present in our lives.
Maybe it's time to sit for a while at some stage today and be
grateful to God for the love we have received and given
in our lives, and for what it has meant to us.

This gospel also has its challenges.
Do we restrict our love?
Are there some people that we are called to love, but about
whom we have decided it's just too hard?
What are the obstacles preventing us from loving more?
Are we too hurt, or selfish, or busy?

What is true for us as individuals is also true for us as a
community. Together we need to ask ourselves: are we trying to
love God without loving our neighbors?
Who are the people we as a community love?
Is it just ourselves?
Are we so caught up in catering to our own needs that we
use all our resources to this end without considering the
needs of the community around us?
Maybe these questions warrant some discussion after Eucharist this morning?

5. Disposing People for Eucharist

The story of Bill and Evelyn has a happy ending. Bill never drank
again. He became involved with A.A. and that was a tremendous
help. But I suspect more important to his recovery, and the fullness of
life that he and Evelyn were able to share, was the love they had for
each other. In loving one another they found the source of Life itself!

In Eucharist we pause to celebrate that source of life revealed to us
in Jesus. In him, God took the time to love us. Through this Eucharist
may we take the time and have the courage to love one another.

D. Polishing the Draft

From the final text below you can see that I changed very little from the first draft. The theology seemed sound and there were no obvious difficult terms. But there are two significant changes. At the beginning of section 2, the highlighting of the discrepancy seemed inadequate. The final form appeared to have more impact.

In section 3, the draft seemed to miss something of the insight that had come from my reflection. It was not clear enough in drawing attention to the fact that in our love for another we actually experience God; and this is what constitutes the "special something" of love. The final form seems to capture this better.

All the other changes were made simply to help the spoken flow of the homily.

It took about ten minutes to deliver.

E. The Final Form

1. Engaging the Audience

Some years ago I was working at the St Vincent de Paul Hostel in Brisbane. Part of the ministry involved visiting the detox unit at the Royal Brisbane Hospital. One afternoon I spent some time with a man by the name of Bill. We got on well right from the start. He was a Catholic and when I mentioned I was a priest it made the conversation even easier. He was a smallish man with a bit of a hunch in his back. He smoked constantly and there was a rasp in his voice that had come from drinking two bottles of methylated spirits a day for the last week or so. He had tried many times to get sober.

I'll never forget his voice nor his eyes that afternoon. His eyes filled with tears as he spoke of what he'd done to his wife and family. There was a genuineness in his voice that almost brought tears to my eyes as I listened to him. But for all the remorse there was little hope. He was almost at the stage of absolute despair.

I had little to offer except to encourage him to come to an A.A. meeting.

I went back the next day to visit Bill. This time Evelyn, his wife, was with him. They were sitting quietly on a bench outside the ward. I sat with them for a little while and eventually both Bill and Evelyn began to talk about the problems the disease had brought into their home. It was a drinking story that spread over twenty years and was filled with all the things that happen in a family ravished by this disease.

At one stage, Bill held his head in his hands and shakily said he thought it might be best if Evelyn left him. He didn't want to hurt her any more.

Without even as much as a pause, Evelyn put her arm around him and said to him: "We've been through some bad times in the past and we've got through. There may be some bad times in the future. But somehow together we'll manage!"

That afternoon I glimpsed true love; and I was profoundly moved.

2. Highlighting the Discrepancy

Love really is what life is all about, but it is also very confusing! There are times when we know we love someone and want to love them more, and yet something within us holds us back, — almost against our will.

If love is so attractive and desirable, why is it that on occasions we find it so hard to reach out in love?

Sometimes we reach our hand out in love towards someone only to draw it back burned, bruised or broken. Maybe it's those hurtful experiences lodged deep in our memories that make us wary in love. Maybe they are the cause of our insulating ourselves against the possible hurt we may experience in loving another.

If this is the case, it is surely costing us dearly!

In many ways, loving plays havoc with personal interests and freedom. To love involves looking to the needs of another rather than concentrating upon our own personal interests.

Like most I've been deeply moved and at times shocked by the television reports of what is happening to the Kurdish people in northern Iraq. No doubt it is a complex political and religious situation, but what is happening there has been influenced by the lust for power of one man. What is being played out on our television screens before our eyes, is a reflection of what may well be happening within our lives.

Within us all there is, if not a lust, at least a strong desire to have our own way. It is this often unconscious inner urge that prevents us from loving. Sometimes to love another appears to have little in it for us and so is not worth the trouble.

A friend once said to me, "It really takes time to be friends!" How simple, and yet how profound! Friendship and love do take time, and time is not something that most of us have a lot of in our busy world. So much of our time is caught up in getting that there is little available for giving. It is not that we plan things that way; it is just the way things seem to be. The pace of our lives may well be the very thing making it hard for us to love.

3. Experiencing the Gospel

"Love God wholeheartedly through loving your neighbor" is Jesus' reply to the Pharisee. Maybe that was what Evelyn was really saying when she said, "We have managed in the past!"

There is something special in loving another and being loved in return. It goes beyond the circumstances of the situation. In love we come to know the bigger picture of life. In love, despite the fact that the odds may seem to be stacked against us, we somehow know that all will be O.K.

One thing the gospel is saying to us today is that when we love another we love God. The words from *Les Miserables* say it so well: "To love another person is to see the face of God".

I guess that is why love is so attractive. In love we know God. We know the source of life itself. We see God face to face. And we are refreshed and energized.

This is what we surrender if we choose not to love.

When the fullness of life is the stake, any cost is worth it.

4. Anticipating the Consequences

Maybe this morning we are being called to pause and reflect upon the loves of our lives.

> To feel again that "something special" at the heart of our relationship with the people we love.
>
> Maybe to see that it is here, at the very core of our being, that God is truly present in our lives.
>
> Maybe it's time to sit for a while at some stage today and be grateful to God for the love we have received and given in our lives, and for what it has meant to us.

> But this gospel also has its challenges.
>
> Do we restrict our love?
>
> Are there some people that we are called to love but have decided it's just too hard?
>
> What are the obstacles preventing us from loving more?
>
> Are we too hurt, or selfish, or busy?

What is true for us as individuals is also true for us as a community. Together we need to ask ourselves: are we trying to love God without loving our neighbors?

> Who are the people we as a community love?
>
> Is it just ourselves?
>
> Are we so caught up in catering to our own needs that we use all our resources to this end without considering the needs of the community around us?
>
> Maybe these questions warrant some discussion after Eucharist this morning?

5. Disposing People for Eucharist

The story of Bill and Evelyn has a happy ending. Bill never drank again. He became involved with A.A. and that was a tremendous help. But I suspect more important to his recovery, and the fullness of life that he and Evelyn were able to share, was the love they had for each other. In loving one another they found the source of Life itself!

In Eucharist we pause to celebrate that source of life revealed to us in Jesus. In him, God took the time to love us. Through this Eucharist may we take the time and have the courage to love one another.

Bibliography

While the manner and order of expression are my own, many of the ideas in this book have been gleaned from a number of different authors. They include the following:

Raymond Brown, "Preaching in Acts of the Apostles" in *A New Look at Preaching*, ed. John Burke, Michael Glazier, Wilmington, DE, 1983.

Kathleen Fischer, *The Inner Rainbow*, Paulist Press, Ramsey, NJ, 1983.

Patrick Collins, *More Than Meets the Eye*, Paulist Press, Ramsey, NJ, 1983.

Eugene Lowry, *Doing Time in the Pulpit*, Abingdon, 1985 and *The Homiletical Plot*, John Knox Press, Atlanta, GA, 1980. The seminal thinking contained in these two works has been a major influence in the development of the method contained in this book.

John Shea, *Stories of God*, Thomas More Press, Chicago, IL, 1978; *Stories of Faith*, Thomas More Press, Chicago, IL, 1980. Shea's work has substantially shaped my thinking with regard to religious experience.

Reginald Fuller, *The Use of the Bible in Preaching*, Fortress Press, Philadelphia, PA, 1981.

O.C. Edwards Jr., *Elements of the Homiletic*, Pueblo Publishing Co., New York, 1982.

George Fitzgerald, *A Practical Guide to Preaching*, Paulist Press, Ramsey, NJ, 1980.

Joe Holland and Peter Henriot, *Social Analysis*, Dove Communications, Melbourne, 1983.

Clare Brissett, *Reflective Living*, Affirmation Books, Natick, MA, 1983.